THE FATHER OF NON-HAN CHINESE LINGUISTICS

LI FANG–KUEI

(1902–1987)

A PIONEER IN THE STUDY OF MINORITY
LANGUAGES IN CHINA
A Chronology/Biography

Compiled by Peter Li

authorHOUSE®

AuthorHouse™
1663 Liberty Drive
Bloomington, IN 47403
www.authorhouse.com
Phone: 1 (800) 839-8640

Published by AuthorHouse 01/17/2017

ISBN: 978-1-5246-0374-8 (sc)
ISBN: 978-1-5246-0373-1 (e)

Library of Congress Control Number: 2016906932

Print information available on the last page.

Any people depicted in stock imagery provided by Thinkstock are models,
and such images are being used for illustrative purposes only.
Certain stock imagery © Thinkstock.

This book is printed on acid-free paper.

Because of the dynamic nature of the Internet, any web addresses or links contained in
this book may have changed since publication and may no longer be valid. The views
expressed in this work are solely those of the author and do not necessarily reflect the views
of the publisher, and the publisher hereby disclaims any responsibility for them.

Dedicated to My Parents

Models of Integrity, Love and Humanity

Fang-Kuei and Hsu Ying in Hawaii, July 1939

"Language is one of the greatest manifestations of the human spirit; there is no study more rewarding."

Li Fang-Kuei

Contents

Preface ix

Chapter I   Childhood and Youth 1902–1924 1

Chapter II   First Trip to America 1924–1929 15

Chapter III Most Productive Years (I) 1929–1937 44

Chapter IV   Interim: Two Years at Yale
             Second Trip to America 1937–1939 85

Chapter V   Most Productive Years (II) 1939–1946 96

Chapter VI   Twenty Years at the University of Washington:
             Third Trip to America 1949–1969 139

Chapter VII Professor Emeritus: In Retirement
             1969–1987 158

Chapter VIII The Legacy of Li Fang-Kuei 193

Epilogue 201

Selected Bibliography 211

Index 215

Preface

Writing this chronology of Li Fang-Kuei and the career that shaped it has been a journey of discovery for me, the son of Li Fang-Kuei. He seldom talked to us, my sisters and me, about his work or his adventures in the field. To be honest, neither did we spend much time asking him about his experiences or his thoughts when he did his fieldwork. He did not keep a detailed diary of his activities as many of his contemporaries did, such as his friend and fellow linguist, Y. R. Chao, at the time. In hindsight, we, his children, should have been more conscientious and curious about his life and career when he was alive; but we missed that golden opportunity. Fortunately, before he passed away in 1987, he was persuaded to participate in an Oral History Project at the University of California, Berkeley, where he left a record of his career as a pioneering linguist in China.

By that time, however, his energy was low and his memory fading. As a consequence, the record was somewhat sketchy. Therefore, in writing this chronology, I needed to comb through his many scholarly writings, the accounts of other scholars, my mother's writings recalling their life together of fifty-five years, and the archives of the Academia Sinica in Taiwan to piece together his life and career as a linguist, scholar, and adventurer in China

Li Fang-Kuei's career in linguistics began in America at the University of Chicago where he studied general linguistics. His professors included Leonard Bloomfield, Carl Darling Buck, and Edward Sapir who, in particular, became Li's advisor and mentor at the University of Chicago. Sapir, one of the foremost linguists in North America, wrote in 1927 that Li Fang-Kuei was the first properly trained Chinese student of linguistics to study and do fieldwork in American Indian languages. In the summer of 1927, Li worked together with Sapir on the language of the Hupa Indians in northern California. After two weeks of training, Sapir sent him out on his own to search out the Mattole Indians and record their language. Later, after Li had completed his Ph.D. dissertation, Sapir sent him out on two more field trips to northern Canada to work with the Chipewyan and Hare Indians. Since then, his findings in the field of American Indian linguistics have been recognized as authoritative.

When Li returned to China in 1929, a position was already waiting for him at the Institute of History and Philology at the newly established Academia Sinica, the most prestigious institution of higher learning in China. Upon arrival there he immediately plunged into his research, which included the study of Archaic Chinese phonology, Sino-Tibetan, and Tai dialects in the provinces of southwest China. His field work took him to remote villages in the provinces of Guangxi, Guizhou, Yunnan, and Sichuan. Throughout his career in China, and later in the United States, he became known in linguistic circles as "The Father of non-Han Chinese Linguistics." "Non-Han" is a term used to refer to mostly non-ethnic Chinese who do not speak one of the seven major dialects of China; they have languages/dialects, cultures, and traditions of their own.

As a graduate student in linguistics at the University of Chicago in 1927, Li was fortunate to have found mentors among the university's legendary team of linguists: Edward Sapir, Carl Darling Buck, and Leonard Bloomfield. It was Sapir who introduced him to American Indian languages and the harsh realities of pursuing these studies. Others helped him learn and absorb 18 languages, including Sanskrit and the old period languages of Persian, Norse, Icelandic, and German, as well as Greek and Latin grammar. He received three American degrees before he returned to China late in 1929. Thus, he was able to apply his extensive training in Indo-European and comparative linguistics to his study of Tai, Sino-Tibetan, and Archaic Chinese.

Li's writings throughout his sixty-some years of scholarship and research showed a remarkable consistency -- his writings were always clear and precise, and his formulations often subtle and understated. His scholarly and academic life exhibited a single-minded devotion to his field of study, never deviating far from it despite the many years that often intervened between his writings on a single topic. His memory about linguistic matters was like a vise. He never forgot the slightest detail related to such matters, even though he was quite absent-minded in his daily life. Because he had a sharp ear and quick ear-hand coordination,, he was able to transcribe the speech of his informants rapidly and accurately, a highly valuable skill before the convenience of recording machines. Li often lamented the fact that contemporary linguistics students rarely wanted to venture into the study of a language that they knew nothing about, something outside their comfort zone, in order to test their analytical abilities.

As early as 1928, Li expressed his interest in studying the languages of southwest China and his desire to train students in fieldwork. Subsequently, his many extensive field trips in the region with his student assistants were the fulfillment of that dream. These trips meant many weeks and months of hardship, living under trying conditions – eating local cuisine at subsistence level, and traveling over dangerous terrain. After working for months under these harsh conditions, besides accumulating a trove of valuable linguistic data, he also came home with an unwelcome case of lice, which infested the hair and clothing of the entire family. My mother often had to soak his clothing in boiling water to get rid of the vermin. The many publications that resulted from Li's pioneering fieldwork have become classics and models for many of his linguistics students, some of whom later became outstanding linguists themselves.

Professor Ting Pang-Hsin wrote about Li Fang-Kuei in this way: "Professor Li was a true Chinese gentleman and scholar. He had scholarly refinement and exhibited a characteristic sincerity, cultivation, and broadmindedness. Also, steeped in the Western critical tradition, Li's scholarly works displayed a meticulous care in formulations, penetrating powers of perception, and subtlety of analysis."

Professor Ronald Scollon, one of Li's later students at the University of Hawaii, commented upon the passing of Li Fang-Kuei in 1987 as "… a loss of the man who had set the standard for diversity of original fieldwork, for meticulous accuracy in representation, for scholarly caution in his theoretical writing, and for his deeply human care for his relationships with colleagues and students."

Probably a question lurking in many people's minds was why Li Fang-Kuei devoted a lifetime to the study of a subject as obscure as linguistic historical reconstruction.. A student once asked him this question; his answer, after a long pause, was, "Language is one of the greatest manifestations of the human spirit; there is no study more rewarding."

Acknowledgement:

It is my pleasure to express my gratitude and appreciation to many who have given me help and advice along the way in the writing of this chronological biography. I wish to express special thanks to a number of individuals. First, to Anne Yue-Hashimoto for suggesting that I write something about my father using chronology as an organizing principle; otherwise I would never have undertaken this project at all. Next, to Ting Pang-Hsin, who wrote a letter of introduction to Wang Fan-sen, then Director of the Institute of History and Philology of the Academia Sinica in Taiwan, who generously opened the archives of the IHP for me and supplied me with valuable information. Also, to Paul Jen-kuei Li, who helped me in many ways as I went through various drafts of the manuscript as well as to Suzie Scollon and the Scollon Estate, for permission to quote extensively from Ron Scollon's *This is What They Say.* The following institutions granted me permission to use materials from their collections: the Regional Oral History Office of the Bancroft Library, for use of "Fang-Kuei Li: Linguistics East and West, American Indian, Sino-Tibetan, and Thai"; *The University of Chicago Magazine*, for authorization to quote from an article by Edward Sapir; the *National Geographic*, for use of maps from the *Atlas of the World* (1999 edition); the Institute of History and Philology of the Academia Sinica, Taiwan, for use of photos and correspondence from its archives.

My thanks to Malca Chall, for her excellent editing of an earlier version of the manuscript. Last but not least, I would like to thank Kathleen Kish who read the entire manuscript and whose interest in subject–matter and thoughtful editing helped render my manuscript much clearer and more readable. For any remaining errors of commission or omission, the responsibility is totally mine. To any reader who would bring to my attention further errors of commission or omission, I would be eternally grateful.

Finally, just for the record, my sister, Lindy, whose wanton threat that I would never finish this chronology, made me more determined to complete the project just to prove her wrong. Thanks sis. My daughters, Jennifer and Caroline, read sections of the chronology as I plugged along and murmured words of encouragement not really knowing where I was going with it. Marjorie read the final version with her critical eye and gave her seal of approval.

Notes on Romanization and Pronunciation

The romanization I have used is a combination of the traditional Wade–Giles system and the Pinyin system used in China today. For the names of many of the older generation of scholars, I have used the traditional Wade–Giles system. For the younger scholars in China, I have used the pinyin system. Hints on pronunciation: in Pinyin, "e" is pronounced like "u" in hug, "x" is pronounced like "sh" in sheet, "c" is pronounced like "t's" like in it's, and "q" is pronounced like "ch" in cheese, "zh" is pronounced like "j" in jerk. In the earlier part of the narrative before 1949 I have used the more traditional "Peking" rather than Beiping or Beijing; after 1949, I use "Beijing." In most cases I have followed the Chinese tradition of placing the surname, or family name, first and then the personal name, usually two syllables. Juxtaposing two systems sometimes creates problems: the family name "Xu" in Pinyin is the same as "Hsu" in Wade-Giles. This is just one example.

Peter Li
December 4, 2016
Walnut Creek
peterli10@yahoo.com

Chapter I.

Childhood and Youth
1902-1924

Childhood and Youth
1902-1924

1902 August 15 Born in Guangzhou, China

Li Fang-Kuei was born in Guangzhou (formerly known as Canton), China, to Li Guangyu and his wife He Zhaoying (née He, the "e" is pronounced like "u" in hug). Li Guangyu was a government official with the title Circuit Intendant of Zhaoyangluo who had earned a *jinshi* degree (the highest level of the imperial examination system) in 1880. He Zhaoying, his wife, was a gifted painter, who had served for several years before her marriage, in the palace of the Empress Dowager Cixi (1835-1908) of the Qing dynasty (1644-1911).

Fang-Kuei was a good-natured child who seldom cried. Perhaps this was so because, in addition to the young nursemaid who was hired to nurse him, the many servants in the household took turns carrying him during the night. Therefore, as it was said, his head never touched a pillow until he was two years old. As he grew older he learned to play mahjong so skillfully that he could occasionally sit in for his father, playing with his father's colleagues while squatting or kneeling on a chair. Fang-Kuei's happy childhood was spent on the spacious premises of the *yamen* (the local

Fig. 1 Fang-Kuei's mother, He Zhaoying, ca. 1925

administrative building and living compound for local officials), with its many courtyards, ponds, and pavilions, seldom venturing outside.

The Li family came from a line of distinguished scholars, several of whom had obtained the *jinshi* degree. Fang-Kuei's grandfather, Li Xilian, was an 1860 *jinshi*; and his father, Li Guangyu, an 1880 *jinshi*, twenty years later. To have two successive generations of the *jinshi* degree in the same family was an unusual accomplishment.

Fang-Kuei's maternal grandfather, He Naiying, was also an 1880 *jinshi*. The two scholar-officials were close friends and considered by custom to be "classmates." When the time came for Li Guangyu to take another wife, He Naiying suggested his daughter He Zhaoying, who, at age 29, was considered past the usual marriageable age. But since this was not Li's first marriage and she was not the only wife, this was considered a good match.

He Zhaoying was a bright, intelligent, and precocious child, who displayed artistic talent when she was quite young. It was not surprising, then, that she was chosen to serve as a painter to the Empress Dowager Cixi. Moreover, even after she had retired from her official position at court, because of her intelligence and resourcefulness, her father kept her at home to run the household. Consequently, she did not marry until age 29, after all her younger sisters were married. She was indeed, as time

Fig. 2 An example of He Zhaoying's painting dated 1924

would tell, a very capable woman. In no time she took charge of the large Li household, despite the grumbling of the other wives and concubines.

1902–1911 A Happy Childhood

The Li family's ancestral home was in Shanxi province in northern China. But since Fang-Kuei was born and spent his early years in Guangzhou, Guangzhou became his childhood home. This explains why Cantonese was close to his first language. Even though his father later returned to Shanxi, Fang-Kuei and his brother and sister went to Peking (known as Beijing after 1949) and never returned to their ancestral home. Fang-Kuei spent nine happy years playing within the spacious *yamen* courtyards with his brothers, sisters, and cousins.

When the family hired a teacher for the older children, Fang-Kuei, still too young to attend class, stood outside the school room listening to his playmates' recitations. When they stumbled and could not remember their lessons, he would whisper the lines to them. Noticing that his son was intelligent beyond his years, his father allowed him to attend class with the older students. Fang-Kuei never had to fret about his lessons like the others; he learned his lessons quickly.

His idyllic days, however, came to an abrupt end in 1911, when the fate of the imperial Qing dynasty was shaken to its foundations by the Republican Revolution of 1911.

1911–1912 Republican Revolution

This was a time of momentous changes in China. During the 19th century, China underwent its steepest decline in dynastic power and prestige ever. The Qing dynasty (1644–1911), having reigned for over 250 years, was in its last gasp as the century was drawing to a close. China had lost two Opium Wars and was forced to sign the "unequal treaties," which opened five treaty ports to foreign trade. The year 1900 saw the birth of a xenophobic group called the Boxers, whose anti-Christian and anti-foreign activities aroused the fear of the foreigners in Peking. In August 1900, some 10,000 allied troops of the eight foreign powers (Britain, France, America, Germany, Italy, Japan, Russia, and Austria-Hungary) fought their way into Peking to end the siege of Peking by the Boxers. The Empress Dowager Cixi fled Peking, and the Boxers were suppressed.

As the first decade of the 20th century drew to a close, discontent with the tottering dynasty became greater and greater. Popular uprisings had plagued the dynasty for decades during the 19th century. These popular uprisings culminated in the Republican Revolution of 1911–12, which finally toppled the Qing dynasty and terminated the more than 2,000-year-old imperial system. Imperial rule ended with the abdication of the "Last Emperor" Puyi on February 12, 1912. Dr. Sun Yat-sen, the father of the republic and the driving force behind the revolution, became the first president of the Republic of China.

1910 March 19 Hsu Ying Born in Tokyo, Japan

On March 19, Hsu Ying, Li Fang-Kuei's future wife, was born in Tokyo, Japan, to Xu Shuzheng (1880-1925), who was later to become a noted general, and his wife Xia Xuan (aka Xia Hongjun, 1878-1955). Because Hsu Ying was born during the cherry blossom season (March/April), she was named "Ying" (Cherry Blossom). Three months after her birth, at the end of Xu Shuzheng's military training in Japan, the family moved back to China. Xu Shuzheng, born in 1880 in the little village of Liquan, some 50 miles from the major city of Xuzhou, came from a humble, scholarly background. His father, Xu Zhiqing, was a well-known teacher of traditional Chinese classical learning in Xuzhou. His son studied with him and developed a reputation as a child prodigy. He could write poetry at age 7 and passed the first imperial examinations at age 13. But he soon gave up traditional Chinese learning for the military. Times were changing. The Qing dynasty was on the verge of collapse; and the Western powers were knocking at China's gates, clamoring for concessions and trading rights after China suffered a number of defeats at their hands.

Fig. 3 Hsu Ying's parents: Mother, Xia Xuan;
Father, Xu Shuzheng

Xu Shuzheng was betrothed to Xia Xuan for 8 years before they were finally married in 1900 after Shuzheng ran off to join the military (*toubi congrong*). When his mother found her son missing, she had him brought back home to be married. The marriage however, did not deter the young man from his military ambitions. In fact, he and his brother-in-law, Xia Hongjun, who was already a military officer, often discussed military matters and how they could help their country. The young bride also supported her husband, encouraging him to join the military. When Xu Shuzheng was sent to Japan to study at the military academy in 1905, Xia Xuan joined her husband, bringing along their two young sons. After returning to China in 1910, the rise of Xu Shuzheng's military career was meteoric.

1912 He Zhaoying Moves to Peking with her Children

Fang-Kuei's mother, He Zhaoying, was an intelligent, strong-willed, and determined woman. After the Revolution of 1911, when her husband, Li Guangyu, decided to retire to his ancestral home in the remote village of Lijiaogou (the Ravine of the Li Family), Shanxi province, she did not accompany him. Instead, she made up her mind to leave her husband and return to Peking with her children. Peking was where she was raised and had lived during the years she served as a court painter. Practically overnight she became a "Single Mom," saddled with the responsibilities of raising her three children on her own. She borrowed some money from her family, bought a house, and rented out part of it to support herself and her children. She was a "superwoman" (*nuqiangren*) ahead of her time. She believed that her children would have the best educational opportunities in Peking because that was where the best schools and universities were. Accordingly, right away she enrolled Fang-Kuei, being the youngest, in the Primary School of Peking Normal College where he would study for the next few years.

1914 Graduates from Primary School

Fang-Kuei graduated from primary school and enrolled in the Peking Normal College Middle School. At the time, Fang-Kuei recalled, he loved to read novels and was not a particularly good student. Every week the students were required to write an essay. His essays never exceeded one written page, but the teacher always gave him high marks. On one particular occasion, his essay was chosen to be displayed on the blackboard and read to the class. The teacher's praise read: "Even though the essay is short, it has substance!" There was another student Wang Shu-lin, who loved to write long essays and took great pride in the fact. But the teacher was not impressed. He once wrote on Wang's essay: "Your essay is overly long and stinky. It is as stinky as stinky tofu." Fang-Kuei and Wang Shu-lin often joked about this many years later.

1919 May 4th Movement

The May Fourth Movement was another momentous event in modern Chinese history following close upon the Revolution of 1911. The movement began as 3,000 students of Peking University protested the Chinese government's acquiescence to the Treaty of Versailles, which gave the German concessions in Shandong province to Japan instead of returning them to China after Germany's defeat in World War I. It soon grew into a nationwide movement, marking the birth and upsurge of Chinese nationalism. At the same time, it evolved into a literary and cultural movement as well, changing the entire intellectual climate of the nation.

It was during this period that Fang-Kuei wrote an inflammatory essay that, had it not been for the intervention of his favorite teacher on his behalf, might have gotten him expelled from school. Li was 17 years old at the time, even though he did not participate in the demonstrations, he must have been influenced by the events of the time.

1920 College Entrance Examinations

In 1920 Li Fang-Kuei graduated from Middle School and began making preparations to take his college entrance examinations. Fang-Kuei and two of his classmates, Zhang Yu-zhe (later a well-known astronomer) and Liu Xi-gu (later a government official), graduated in the same year and decided to take the college entrance examinations together. Liu heard that Qinghua College offered its graduates the opportunity to study in America on a government scholarship. For that reason, Qinghua became their first choice. They also decided to apply to Beiyang College of Engineering in Tianjin, and finally Peking Union Medical College, just in case they failed to get into Qinghua.

The first examination was for Beiyang College of Engineering. All three passed the examination. Next they took the Qinghua entrance examinations, which were given mostly in English. Two of the exams were on health and woodworking, fields which they knew nothing about; another was on geography, and another on mathematics—all in English. Only Chinese literature and history were examined in Chinese. To prepare for the exams the three 18-year-olds scraped together enough money to buy some books on math and geography; they also borrowed a book on health. They studied together, testing each other. Ultimately this method worked; all three passed their entrance examinations. Having achieved their goal, they decided to skip the Peking Union Medical College exam and entered Qinghua College.

1920-24 Four Years at Qinghua

Fang-Kuei registered as a pre-med student at Qinghua College, intending to study medicine. But when he took a course on Latin, taught by a famous Latin professor, he was hooked. He also took courses in German, This was the beginning of his interest in linguistics. After two years of study at Qinghua, the school wanted to confirm his intended major field of study. By this time, Li had already decided to change his field from pre-med to linguistics.

His next big decision was to choose a university in America. He chose the University of Michigan. The conventional wisdom of the time was to avoid famous universities such as Harvard, Yale, Chicago, or Columbia, because they were located in large, bustling cities, where it was easy for new students to be distracted. A small American town was considered to be a more conducive environment for a new foreign student. The University of Michigan, a mid-sized university in the American Midwest, located in the small town of Ann Arbor, with a good program in linguistics, seemed the ideal choice.

Chapter II.

First Trip to America
1924-1929

First Trip to America
1924-1929

1924-1926 Li Attends the University of Michigan

After graduating from Qinghua College in 1924 at age twenty-two, Fang-Kuei left China for the first time, sailing across the Pacific to study in America. It was an emotional moment for his mother, He Zhaoying, when it was time to bid farewell to her youngest and favorite child. She did not know how long he would be overseas (*piaoyang guohai*), but she knew that she must let him go because it was important for his future. After three weeks at sea, Li arrived in America, took a train to Ann Arbor, Michigan, and enrolled at the University of Michigan. Since Qinghua was a preparatory college at the time, providing the equivalent of two years of college, Li was able to register at the junior year level.

At Michigan, Li continued his study of Latin literature, reading the famous dramatists and poets, Virgil, Plautus, Terence, and Catullus. In addition, he studied extensively with the distinguished Professor Samuel Moore, co-author with Thomas A. Knott of *Elements of Old English*, taking his Old English and Middle English dialects. Meanwhile, his study of German philology, Gothic, and Middle-High German strengthened his background in German.

Philosophy became a new field of interest for Fang-Kuei. He also took courses in poetics. Years later, he spoke with pride about his prize-winning paper, *"Laocoön: An Essay on the Limits of Painting and Poetry* by G.E. Lessing (1729-1781)." He read Lessing's text on aesthetics in the original German, whereas his classmates could read it only in English translation. At the end of his two years of undergraduate study, Fang-Kuei had gained a superior knowledge of Latin, the history of the English language, and German.

His two years at Michigan must have been an exciting time for him. The University of Michigan was then a mid-sized university in the Midwestern town of Ann Arbor. While there, he completed the course requirements in linguistics, accumulating an outstanding record. He graduated with "High Distinction" and was inducted into the Phi Beta Kappa Honor Society. Like a typical American college student, Fang-Kuei also went to cheer on the Wolverines at Saturday afternoon football games and attended concerts given by the Music department of the university.

1926-1927 Enrolls at the University of Chicago

After graduating from the University of Michigan in 1926, Fang-Kuei enrolled in the fall at the University of Chicago in the Linguistics Department to study with professors Edward Sapir, Leonard Bloomfield, and Carl Darling Buck. Li had decided early on that he intended to study with the best linguists in the field; it did not really matter to him what specific material they taught. He just wanted to study with the best.

It was probably during registration for new students in Mandel Hall that Li met Professor Edward Sapir for the first time. And Fang-Kuei had a special request: he asked for permission to register for Sapir's Introduction to Linguistics, at the same time, registering for Buck's course of the same name. Sapir, however, did not object. He said, "OK, you can take that course too, because we probably will talk about very different things." Li therefore took both introductory courses in the same term, something that might be frowned upon by less generous professors. In his years at Chicago, Fang-Kuei also studied Sanskrit, Old Persian, Avestan, Lithuanian, Old Bulgarian, and Old Church Slavic. Rounding out his study of Indo-European linguistics, he also took comparative Greek and Latin grammar, with Carl Darling Buck; and German syntax and morphology, with Leonard Bloomfield.

Li was a diligent student at Chicago. In Buck's class on Greek and Latin grammar, he said, "I took very careful notes of Buck's lectures. I have a stack of little cards, notes which he gave in the lecture. Later on, he published his book, *Comparative Greek and Latin Grammar* . . . I looked at my cards. They are exactly what are published in that book." (Li 1988) Li also studied many of the other exotic Indo-European languages that Buck taught, including Old Persian and Aveston.

After one quarter of study at the University of Chicago, Li was noticed by his professor, Edward Sapir, who wrote on a slip of paper, "I have a clever Chinaman in my class," which he or a colleague left in a book in the university library found many years later by Fang-Kuei's colleague. He began to take a special interest in this quiet Chinese student, who had exceptional linguistic abilities. Soon, Sapir took Li under his wing, and became his mentor. Li recalled:

With Sapir, I spent much more time, because out of the class he was very chatty. He talked about Sino-Tibetan, about Burmese, about Thai, about Tibetan . . . He would often refer me to read some of the publications . . . . on Chinese. "Have you read Karlgren's Phonologie Chinoise? . . . . *Have you read Maspero's* Le Dialecte de Changan? *I said, "No, I haven't read that yet." He said, "Well, you better read that."*

He would assign all these things for me to read on Sinology, and then he asked me to read books on Thai grammar. He was particularly interested in Tibetan. He said, "There are lots of books on Tibetan in the library. You can take a look at that. There is a famous Tibetanist in Chicago. He is the curator of the Chicago Museum. Mr. Laufer." He said, "You can try to contact him to see if he has anything to say." (Li 1988: 12)

Fang-Kuei also spent a year studying German syntax and morphology with Leonard Bloomfield. Whereas Sapir was a gifted lecturer, Bloomfield was not. Sapir was fluent, articulate, and elegant. Often students from other fields would come to sit in on his classes just to hear him lecture. Bloomfield, by contrast, was not a good lecturer. There were only three students in his class on Germanic Phonology and Word Formation. In the next quarter, Fang-Kuei was the only student left in the class. For his final paper in the course, Bloomfield asked Li to write on the use of case in Old English. Since he knew Fang-Kuei studied Old English, he said, "You read Old English; read King Alfred's *Pastoral Care*, which is about two volumes. You read that, and see if you find anything about the Germanic use of case in Old English." So Li began reading *Pastoral Care*, which was the oldest known book written in English. After two weeks of study, he reported back something about Old English's use of the genitive case that looked interesting. After more reading, Li wrote a short outline of what he had found. Bloomfield thought it was very interesting and asked Li if he would like to write his dissertation on the subject. But, by that time, Li had already completed his dissertation on Mattole with Sapir.

Sapir, a member of the Anthropology Department at Chicago, taught courses on phonetics, field methods, and American Indian languages. After Fang-Kuei took his course on phonetics, Sapir asked him if he would like to study American Indian languages. This was exactly the invitation Li was hoping for; he couldn't wait to get out in the field and learn how to conduct a live investigation.

In the meanwhile, to get acquainted with the field of American Indian linguistics, Sapir asked Li to look at his field notes on the Sarcee language. He told Li, "You can work on my Sarcee materials. You go ahead and see what you can do with them." Fang-Kuei studied Sapir's field notes and, by spring 1927, brought back a 50-page report: "A Study of Sarcee Verb-Stems." Sapir was pleased with the result and accepted it as Fang-Kuei's master's thesis. It was published in 1930 in the *International Journal of American Linguistics.*

On February 11, 1927, Sapir wrote to his colleague, Alfred Kroeber, at the University of California, Berkeley, that the American Council of Learned Societies just received a five-year grant of $10,000 per year from the Carnegie Corporation for the study of American Indian linguistics. Further on in the same letter, he mentioned he had a "thoroughly excellent student" in his class who would be a good candidate to work on Athabaskan linguistics: "…I have at least one thoroughly excellent student, a Chinese Boxer Indemnity man named Li, who has a good ear, tremendously enthusiastic and assimilative capacity, and a good sense of form. He should certainly be given a chance in the Athabaskan field, for he has been learning Sarcee and Navaho …" (Sapir 1927)

Fig. 4 Edward Sapir (1884–1939), Fang-Kuei's
Teacher and Mentor

Finally, in the last paragraph of the letter, Sapir mentioned his proposed Hupa project for the summer of 1927, which he hoped would be funded by the Laura Spelman Foundation, in which case, he wrote, "…I may have Li [come] along too for continued training and perhaps set him to work on some other Pacific Athabaskan dialect…"

On May 9, 1927, Sapir wrote to Franz Boas at Columbia University, recommending that Fang-Kuei be considered for appointment as Research Assistant in the Linguistics Department at the University of Chicago: "He [Fang-Kuei] has just completed an excellent paper entitled "A Study of the Sarcee Verb-stems" for his master's thesis, I hope to see [it] published later on." (Sapir 1927)

Upon Sapir's recommendation, Fang-Kuei's appointment was approved by the Committee on Research in American Indian languages and he was officially designated Research Assistant in the Department of Linguistics at the University of Chicago. In the summer of 1927 Li followed his teacher, Edward Sapir, to northern California to take part in his first field expedition to work with the Hupa Indians.

1927 Summer Learns Field Methods in Northern California

The summer of 1927 marked an important turning point for Fang-Kuei's linguistic career, as he accompanied Sapir to California. Their first stop was at the University of California, Berkeley, where Sapir made a visit to his fellow anthropologist and colleague, Alfred Kroeber, to obtain information about the Hupa Indians in Humboldt County. Sapir and his student then took the train from Berkeley to Eureka, where they stayed in a high-class hotel in order to take care of some administrative matters.

In the 1920s anti-Chinese sentiment was still running high in California. There had been a shooting between rival "tong" gangs in Eureka's Chinatown in 1885. A Eureka city councilman, David Kendall, age 56, was shot and killed in the crossfire. This led to angry protests; later that day 600 townspeople jammed into the town hall and decided to expel the Chinese from Eureka's Chinatown within 24 hours. Some twenty years later, in 1906, there was another similar but much smaller expulsion in Eureka. Therefore, when it was learned that a Chinese man was going to do fieldwork in Humboldt County, Fang-Kuei had to get a special authorization from the government to carry out his research.

After receiving permission, Sapir and his student took a bus to the Hupa Valley where the Indian Reservation was. For the next two weeks, Fang-Kuei worked with Sapir to learn field methods *in situ*. Li recalled:

He [Sapir] didn't lecture. He'd just sit there, I'd sit there, and the informant would sit here. He'd ask, "How do you say this? How do you say that? How do you say 'I am gone'? 'He is gone'?" All those grammatical points. The Indian would just translate that, the questions, and he and I, both of us, started out writing our own notes. He didn't ask me whether I got it or not. [laughs] . . .

That's the way—some of the techniques you learn by asking questions. So for two weeks – we worked from about 9-12 in the morning and 2-5 in the afternoon every day, and in the evening we would look at our notes and file our cards. It was a very tedious day, and in the summer, the Hupa Valley is like Sacramento Valley in the summer: it is very hot. So after a couple of weeks, he said, "We will take a rest." I said, "I thought we never took a rest!"

Anyway, he said, "Let us take a walk to a nearby Indian village." So we walked to that village, and we found an Indian lady who spoke the Yurok Indian language. So: "We'll take a rest and learn some of that." [laughs] So we started asking similar questions about the Yurok language. . .(Li 1988:14-5)

After two weeks of intensive training, Fang-Kuei left Sapir and went on his own to search for the Mattole Indians, who were supposed to be close to extinction. He went first to Fortuna, hired a taxi, and began to look for the one or two surviving Mattole Indians. It turned out to be a wild goose chase. He was informed that the Mattoles might be further south in Petrolia along the Mattole River.

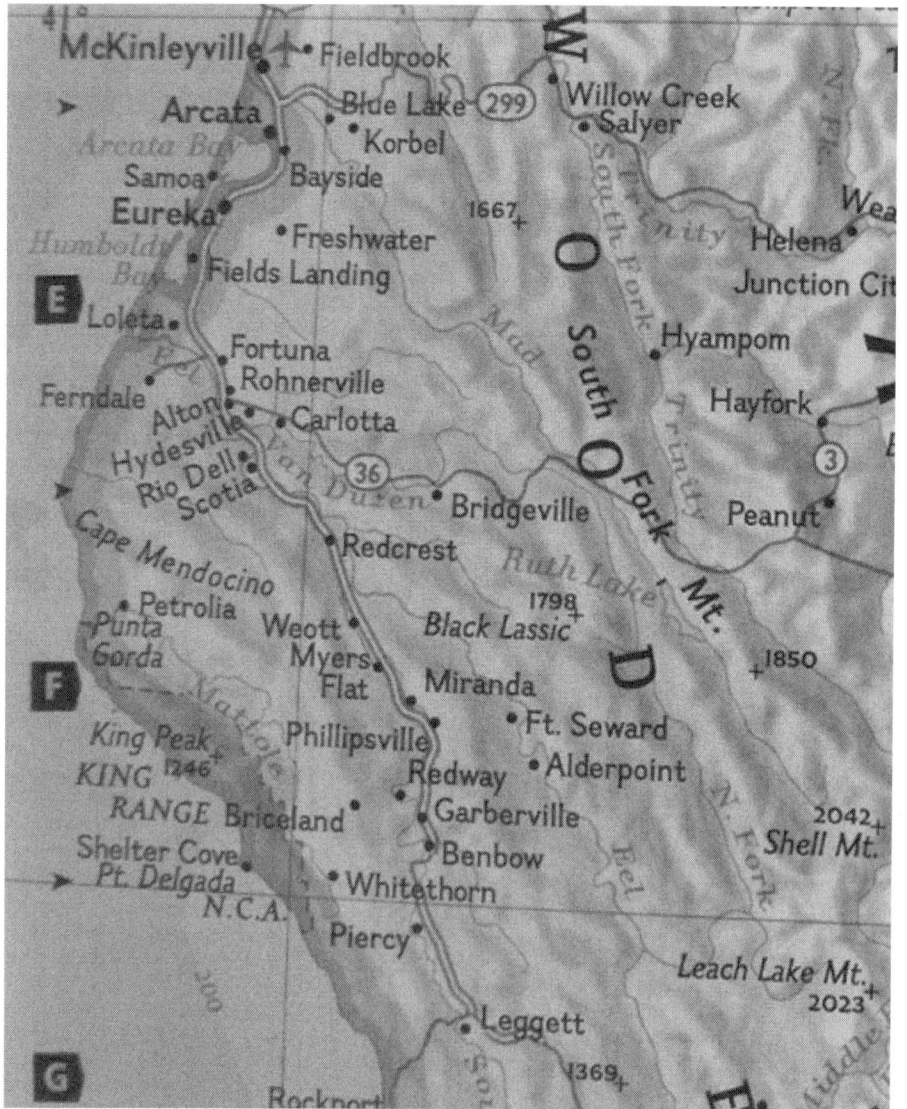

Fig. 5 Northern California where Fang-Kuei did his first fieldwork. (Courtesy of National Geographic)

He then proceeded to Petrolia and learned that the two surviving Indians were still further downstream, near the mouth of the river. This meant going downstream another ten miles. Finding this impossible to do on foot, he spoke to a local farmer and borrowed an old horse (because Li did not know how to ride) from him and rode downstream, where he eventually succeeded in locating the last two surviving Mattole-speaking Indians—a father and son.

The father was an old man in his seventies and already blind, but the son, Isaac Duncan, in his forties or fifties, still in good health, remembered the Mattole language. Fang-Kuei engaged him as his informant, asked him to come to his hotel in Petrolia, and worked with him every day for a month. The informant was not particularly interesting, according to Li, because he did not know how to tell stories. Nevertheless, after a month of intensive work, Fang-Kuei succeeded in recording the Mattole language and preserved for posterity an almost extinct Indian language. His study of the Mattole language became Fang-Kuei's Ph.D. dissertation which was published in 1930 by the University of Chicago Press.

Fig. 6 Li Fang-Kuei at the University of Chicago in 1927.
(Courtesy of *The University of Chicago Magazine*)

After completing his work on Mattole, following his teacher's example, Fang-Kuei visited another Athabaskan Indian tribe, the Wailaki, in Round Valley also in Mendocino County. He found an old man called Old Tip who became his informant. Fang-Kuei worked with him for another month, recorded his language, which he did not find particularly interesting because, according to Li, there were no unusual sounds. Sapir and Li returned to Chicago after a challenging and fruitful summer.

In the fall of 1927 after returning from his summer expedition to the Hupa Valley with his research assistant, Li Fang-Kuei, Edward Sapir wrote about his experience in an article in *The University of Chicago Magazine*, No. 20 (November 1927). Aside from describing his work with the Hupa Indians, Sapir wrote about Fang-Kuei Li, as being "for the first time in the history of linguistic science that a properly trained Chinese student has studied an American Indian language in the field." First, Sapir spent some time explaining the importance of working with the Hupa Indians and then described Li's activities:

...Mr. Li stayed with me long enough to acquaint himself thoroughly with field methods and then left to follow up a few clues that we had obtained that might lead to the discovery of the Mattole language, an Athabaskan dialect that was supposed to be extinct. Very fortunately Mr. Li succeeded in finding an Indian at the mouth of the Mattole River, in the southern part of Humboldt County, who remembered a great deal of this

distinctive Athabaskan dialect, though he had not spoken it for over thirty years. **This means that Mr. Li was able to rescue for science a language that will probably prove to be of very considerable importance in reconstructing the original features of the whole Athabaskan group—no mean feat for a first field trip. In the latter part of the summer Mr. Li proceeded to Round Valley reservation, where he made a record of the Wailaki language, another Athabaskan dialect.** [Emphasis added by editor]. *The combined party, therefore, succeeded in making a rather complete and adequate record of no less than three Athabaskan languages in the course of the summer's work."* (Sapir 1927: 10-11)

1928 June Fang-Kuei Receives his Ph.D. from the University of Chicago

Three months after returning to Chicago from his field trip to California, Fang-Kuei completed writing up the results of his study of the Mattole language. Around Christmas time, he turned in his 150-page study to Professor Sapir, who was so delighted that he suggested that Fang-Kuei submit it as his Ph.D. dissertation. But Li had not yet even applied for admission to the doctoral program. Sapir advised him to begin the process immediately by going to the Registrar to register for his degree and to see about fulfilling the language requirements in German and French. Even after this, however, he was required to wait for six months before he could receive his degree.

Since Li had taken all the graduate-level linguistics courses offered at Chicago, and since his dissertation was already completed, the faculty of the Department, consisting of Buck, Bloomfield, and Sapir, granted him a Rockefeller Fellowship to study for six months at Harvard University.

While at Harvard, from January to June, 1928, Fang-Kuei studied Sanskrit and Tibetan with Professor Walter E. Clark and Visiting Professor Stael von Holstein, who was working on Buddhist Sanskrit texts with Tibetan and Chinese translations. There were a total of four people in the class, two Harvard professors, one other student, and Fang-Kuei.

When Fang-Kuei returned to Chicago in June, he expected to receive his doctoral degree. Sapir however, was not quite yet done with his favorite student. During the summer of 1928, he sent Fang-Kuei on another assignment: to study the Chipewyan language, in northern Alberta, Canada.

1928 Summer Field Work with Chipewyan Indians in Canada

Fang-Kuei arrived at Ft. Chipewyan in late June and sought out François Mandeville (1878-1952), regarded as the best possible informant for this important project. He was the best interpreter, the best storyteller, and the most knowledge-able person in the region. He was also fluent in French. Li

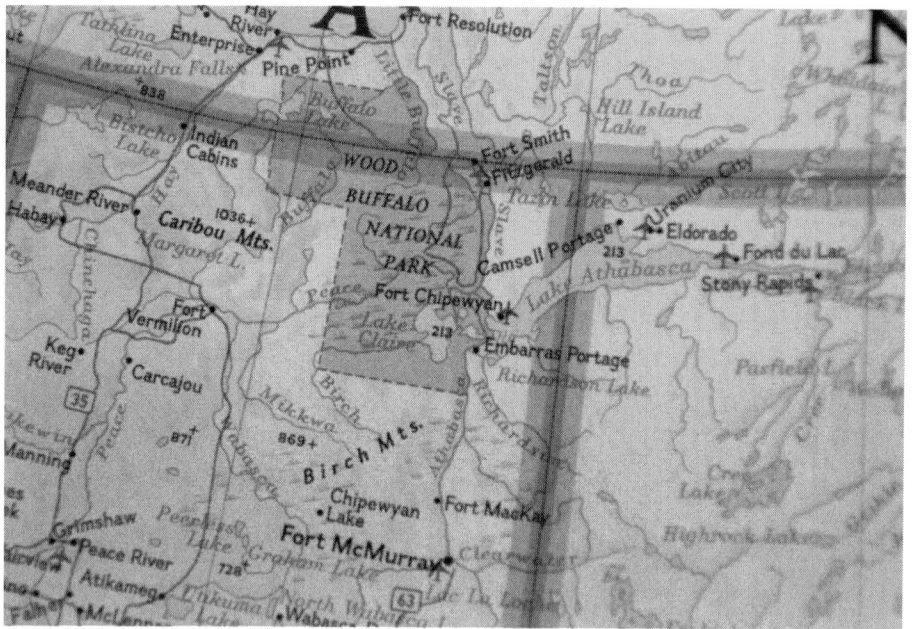

Fig. 7 Ft. Chipewyan in northern Alberta, Canada.
(Courtesy of *National Geographic*)

In the end, Fang-Kuei recorded 21 stories and narratives of the Chipewyan Indians. In 2009 these Chipewyan stories were redacted into literary form by Ron Scollon, a student of Fang-Kuei's in the 1970s at the University of Hawaii. Scollon, having revisited the site where Li had worked, gave a detailed account of Li's methodology and work schedule:

Edward Sapir had a reason, back in 1928, for sending his brilliant young student to Fort Chipewyan. At that time the use of phonemic tone in Athabaskan languages was poorly understood. Sapir felt that a Chinese linguist who already spoke two modern Chinese languages—Mandarin and Cantonese— would be perfectly suited to understand the way tone worked in Northern Athabaskan languages. …

For about six weeks Li and Mandeville met in Mandeville's house to work eight hours a day for six days a week. Li wanted to get enough material for linguistic analysis so he could produce a relatively exhaustive description of the Chipewyan language with a special focus on tone. Mandeville had at least two goals. One was to learn to write Chipewyan—and of course other languages—using Li's phonetic-phonemic orthography. His other goal, with which this book is concerned, was to use this occasion to make a comprehensive collection of the best Chipewyan stories. Li's many publications on Chipewyan and Athabaskan make it clear that he achieved his goal. The stories in this book make it clear that Mandeville also achieved his goal of creating a narrative ethnography of the Chipewyan people.

In the course of their six weeks together they produced ten notebooks of stories. All the stories are included here. The notebook series were made in two stages. In the first stage, Li recorded Mandeville's narration as quickly as possible given the constraints of dictation. This is the upper line of the transcription, in Chipewyan. At the conclusion of each story, they returned to the beginning. Li read the transcription in Chipewyan a few words at a time, giving Mandeville the opportunity to make corrections.

Then Li queried each word to make a word-by-word translation into English. Mandeville gave these word-by-word translations either in English or French. Li recorded only the English result of what was sometimes a double translation -- Chipewyan to French, French to English.

But in addition to the word-by-word translations, they worked to get the best paradigmatic sets they could achieve for each word. In practical terms they focused on verb stems. For example, for each verb translated in as "he became [a wolf]." Li asked for and Mandeville gave forms for 'I became a wolf,' 'you became a wolf,' 'we became wolves,' and so forth. Li also recorded forms such as 'he is becoming a wolf,' 'he will become

Fig. 8 François Mandeville (left) ca. 1912 at Ft. Smith.
(Courtesy of the Scollon Estate)

a wolf.' Li wrote these paradigms on 4"x6" sheets. These are the 2,800 file cards I have mentioned. The two men considered a story completed only when the file slips and the two strands of text in the notebooks were finished." (Scollon 2009:234–236)

On Scollon's visit to Fort Chipewyan, he was able to piece together some interesting details about Li's expedition there. An important source of information was Philip Mandeville, the son of François Mandeville. Mandeville, senior, had built a house at Fort Chipewyan, next to the Athabasca Café and across the road from the Hudson Bay Company. Mandeville and Li met in this house for their work. Philip, who was 25 at the time, listened quietly all day long from upstairs, while his father and Li were working downstairs. Philip informed Scollon that his father read a great deal. He also said that Mandeville's main way of learning stories was to stand by the woodstove in his various stores and trade stories with the old people who came in. About Mandeville, it was said, "He could talk on any subject with the best of them." According to South Coblin, professor at the University of Iowa and Fang-Kuei's former student at the University of Washington, Li had great respect for Mandeville. In fact, he reported, Li referred to only one other person besides Edward Sapir as "my teacher," and that was François Mandeville. (Coblin 2000: 370)

1928 July Founding of the Institute of History and Philology of the Academia Sinica

While Fang-Kuei was earning his Ph.D. in Chicago, the Chinese government was in the process of creating the Academia Sinica. The establishment of this academy in 1928 was a milestone in the Nationalist Government's effort to promote scholarship and research on a national scale, and it soon became the most prestigious academic institution of higher learning in China. The Academia Sinica was to play an important role in the career of Li Fang-Kuei, who became a member in 1929 and remained devoted to it for the rest of his life. The moment he set foot back in China in November of that year, he was invited to become a Research Fellow in its Institute of History and Philology. Thanks to the fact that his reputation had preceded his return to China and to the happy coincidence of the inauguration of the Academia Sinica, Fang-Kuei landed in the ideal place to launch his career as a young scholar.

Strange as it may seem, the Institute of History and Philology was actually formed earlier than the parent organization itself. The Institute was the brain child of Fu Ssu-nien, who was recruited by Ts'ai Yuan-p'ei as a member of the planning committee for establishment of the Academia Sinica. Ts'ai wanted the first branch of the academy to be an Institute of Psychology; but Fu, using his persuasive power and forceful personality, convinced Ts'ai that it was more important to start with an Institute of History and Philology. His argument was that these subject matters, despite their long tradition in China, were being held back by tradition. To combat this, Fu wanted to introduce Western methods of investigation and a more "scientific" approach. After three months of deliberations, the Institute of History and Philology was formally founded in July, 1928. The new Institute was temporarily housed at Sun Yatsen University in Guangzhou (aka Canton) where Fu Ssu-nien was teaching at the time, and, incidentally, had earlier founded a similar institute.

1928 December 18 Fang-Kuei Declares His Intention to Return to China

On December 18, 1928, Li Fang-Kuei wrote to his friend and senior alumnus of Qinghua College, Zhuang Zexuan (1895–1976), who was teaching at Sun Yat-sen University at the time. Zhuang was an educator and studied psychology in America. In his letter Li expressed for the first time his interest in studying dialects in southwest China. He wrote: "I am now very much interested in a survey of the Chinese dialects, particularly of the South, and also in [undertaking] a comparative study of the Sinitic Language in which nothing really scientific has been done." The letter reads:

I have been studying Indo-European philology at the University of Chicago, but have enlarged my field so that I made quite a study of the American Indian languages. I was sent out twice by the Committee on American Indian Research of the American Council of Learned Societies to survey the Indian languages in California and in Northern Canada. A part of my material will be published by the University of Chicago Press under the title Mattole, An Athabaskan Language. *I shall present you a copy of it when it appears.*

... I am wondering what university is interested now in establishing a department of general linguistics, where students could be trained to carry out research and to teach more intelligently foreign as well as the native language.

I hope to travel in Europe for 3 months and return to Canada, where I am requested to make another survey of the Indian languages around the Arctic Circle during the summer.

I shall be very glad to hear from you about yourself and about the university, and in particular about teaching opportunities in any line of work. If there is any opportunity, will you kindly make a recommendation? I shall appreciate it very much. I am supplying you enclosed with a brief record of mine." (Li 1928)

On May 8, 1929, Zhuang Zexuan wrote to Fu Ssu-nien, the newly appointed Director of the Institute of History and Philology, recommending that Li Fang-Kuei be appointed a research fellow at the Institute.

At the completion of his European travels, Fang-Kuei wrote to Fu Ssu-nien from the Windsor Hotel on Dominion Square in Montreal, on June 11, 1929. The purpose of Li's letter was to inform Fu of his intention to return to China once he had finished his summer of field work with the Hare Indians in Northern Canada. At the same time he acknowledged receipt of the appointment letter from the Institute of History and Philology of the Academia Sinica. Finally, he announced that he would depart Canada on October 17th and arrive in China on November 1, 1929.

Around the same time, Li also wrote to Y.R. Chao, to thank him for having sent a copy of his new book, *Studies in Wu Dialects.* Li praised this volume "as the best survey that has been done in China. Its phonetic accuracy and systematic arrangement will make it an indispensable book to all students of Sinitics." In the same letter, Fang-Kuei commented on the appropriateness of the use of the term "Sinitics" to refer to the study of Chinese language and dialects.

1929 Spends Three Months Traveling in Europe

In February Fang-Kuei began his three-month European tour, including France, England, and Germany. He brought with him two letters of introduction from Franz Boas to scholars in Germany. He met the German musicologist, von Hornbostel, who showed Fang-Kuei a wax cylinder recording machine. Later Li purchased one of these machines and brought it back with him to China, where it was to prove useful in his field.

To complement his reading knowledge of the German language, Fang-Kuei took classes in spoken German. At the

University of Berlin he looked up Walter Simon, who was Lecturer in Chinese. The two men got along well and became life-long friends because of their common interest in Tibetan and Chinese. They also had a good time gossiping about Bernhard Karlgren (1889-1978), the pioneer Swedish sinologist, whose groundbreaking work on Chinese philology opened a new era in sinology. It was said that he often discouraged students from studying Chinese philology.

1929 Summer Field Work with the Hare Indians in Canada's Northwest Territories

In June, after his three-month stint in Europe, Fang-Kuei returned to Chicago. Very soon thereafter he set out on the most challenging field trip of his career so far. Under Sapir's instruction, he was to study the language of the Hare Indians in the wilderness of the Northwestern Territories in Canada. The Hare Indians, a hardy Athabaskan group, lived in the village of Ft. Good Hope, north of the Arctic Circle. It took Li three weeks to go from Edmonton, Alberta, to Ft. Good Hope by boat down the McKenzie River. Ft. Good Hope was a trading post of the Hudson Bay Company. Upon arrival, he learned that all of the Indians had gone north, further down the river to an island to catch as much fish as they could to stock up for the winter months. Not one to abandon an assignment, he resolved to follow the Indians to the island. There he found a good informant, camped out on the island, and recorded their Hare language.

Isolated on the island, Fang-Kuei lived in a tent, which the Indians helped him put up, and tried to survive on canned food, eggs, and fish for the duration of his research. However, his canned food rations soon ran out, and the 100 eggs he brought with him began to rot. Now he had to survive on fish alone: "Fish for dinner, fish for breakfast, and fish for lunch." After three months of fieldwork under harsh conditions, Fang-Kuei had enough data and began to make his way back to Chicago. However, since the return trip was going up the McKenzie River, against the current, the trip took longer than expected. The boat headed upstream but was pushed back again and again. Finally, the boat had to be towed to its destination. It is ironic that after all the hardship suffered by Fang-Kuei on this trip, the linguistic materials that he had assembled during his field work in the summer of 1929, for some unknown reason, were never published. Most likely the materials were lost during the World War II after Fang-Kuei's return to China.

On October 17, 1929, after completing his research with the Hare Indians, Fang-Kuei left from Vancouver, B.C., on his way to China, thus concluding his five-year stay in North America.

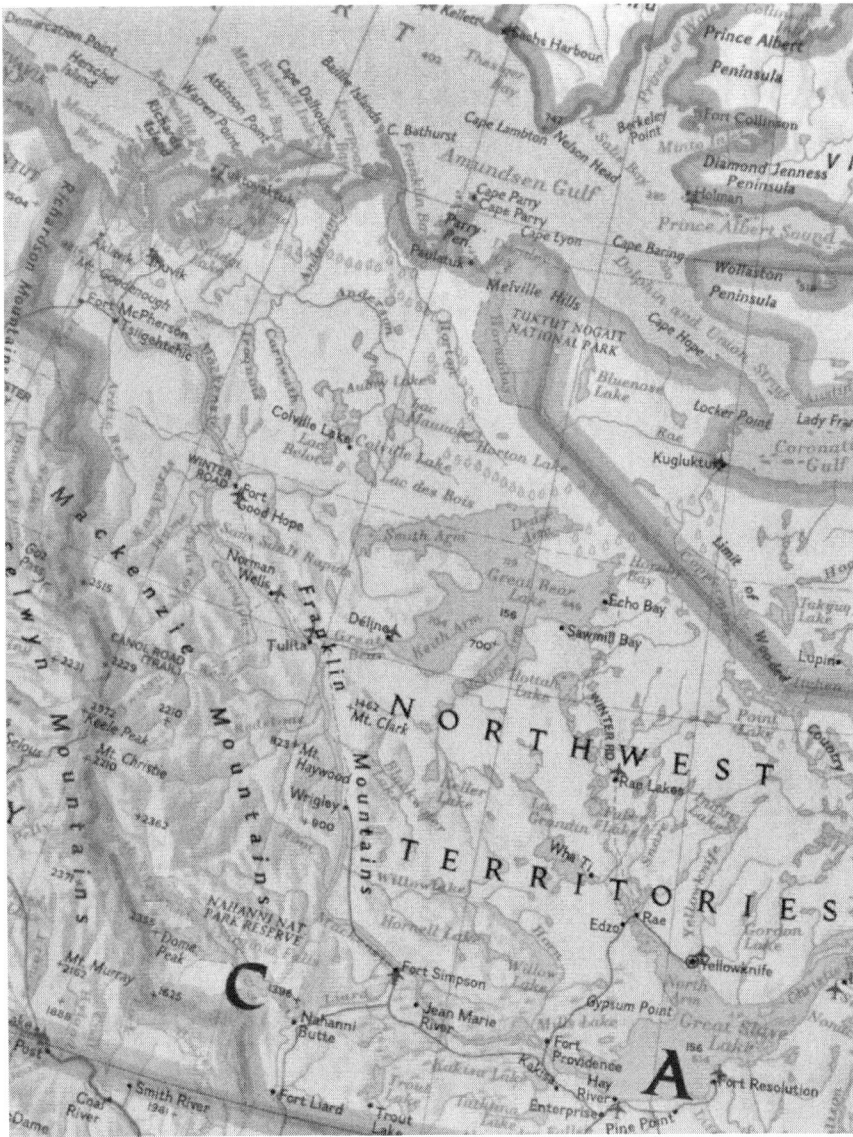

Fig. 9 Ft. Good Hope, Northwest Territories of Canada,
Summer of 1929 (Courtesy of *National Geographic*)

Chapter III.

Most Productive Years (I)
1929-1937

Most Productive Years (I)
1929-1937

1929 November 1. Appointment as Research Fellow of Academia Sinica

Upon his arrival in Shanghai on November 1, Fang-Kuei was met by a representative of Ts'ai Yuan-p'ei, head of the Academia Sinica, who accompanied him to Cangzhou Hotel. Fu Ssu-nien, the newly appointed Director of the Institute of History and Philology, was also staying there. Next day Fang-Kuei was invited to Ts'ai's home for dinner, where he met with Yang Xingfo (an administrative officer of the Academia Sinica), Fu, and Li Siguang (a geologist) to discuss the specifics of the newcomer's role in the recently formed Institute of History and Philology. Li and Fu had already corresponded a few times before this meeting while Li was in Canada.

On their first meeting, Fu asked Li what he knew about Chinese phonology. Li answered frankly that he did not know much about it, since he had been studying Indo-European and American Indian linguistics; but he promised that he would look into it. This lack of knowledge about Chinese phonology, however, did not prevent him from being appointed a full-time research fellow in the Institute of History and Philology.

At first Fang-Kuei was hesitant about accepting the position because he was holding a fellowship from the Rockefeller Foundation. He did not want to be accused of holding two positions and double-dipping. His colleagues, however, persuaded him to accept the appointment because it would facilitate his research travels in China, particularly to the remote parts of the country, where authorization and protection might be needed. The Academia Sinica could provide both. Therefore, he accepted the appointment, but declined the salary for the first year while he held the Rockefeller Fellowship. Years later Fang-Kuei's colleagues would still joke with him that he brought his own "dowry" when he joined the Academia Sinica.

Next, Fang-Kuei exercised his filial affection, by traveling north to Peking to pay respects to his mother, He Zhao-ying, whom he had not seen for five years. It must have been a happy and tearful reunion; it was probably shocking for him to see how much his mother had aged during the intervening years. While there, he also met Y.R. Chao (1892-1982) for the first time, even though the two men had already corresponded with each other. Chao was Fang-Kuei's senior colleague by ten years and had already begun his study of and research into Chinese dialects. Recognizing Li's potential, he had recommended him to Fu and Ts'ai for an appointment in the Academia Sinica. Later Chao and Fang-Kuei were to collaborate in studying Chinese dialects.

Fig. 10. Li Fang-Kuei and Y.R. Chao meeting in Peking
for the first time. ca. 1929

1929 Meets Hsu Ying for the First Time and a Three-year Long Courtship

As a recently returned student from America with an advanced degree from a distinguished university and an appointment to the Academia Sinica, Li Fang-Kuei became one of the most eligible bachelors in town. Y.R. Chao and his wife, Yang Bu-wei, invited Fang-Kuei to dinner, hoping to match him up with their niece. Later Ding Wen-jiang (1887-1936), a well-known geologist, issued a similar invitation, motivated by the wish to introduce him to their adopted daughter. However, nothing came of these meetings.

Soon news leaked that Fang-Kuei had a girlfriend. Her name was Hsu Ying, daughter of the noted general Xu Shuzheng (1880-1925). Hsu Ying was to become his wife of fifty-five years and the most important person in his life after his mother.

Fang-Kuei courted the young woman for three long years before he finally received the approval of her family. On their first date, they were chaperoned by Hsu Ying's older brother, Hsu Shen-chiao and his wife, *née* Wang. On that occasion Fang-Kuei invited them to dine at the famous Peking restaurant Yuhuatai. This was a time-honored restaurant in

Fig. 11. Fang-Kuei and Hsu Ying at #9 Great Sweet
Water Well Street in Peking

Peking, founded in early 1921 and offering Jiangsu cuisine. Some of the featured dishes included braised shredded chicken with ham and dried bean curd, sautéed eel tail, deep-fried fish and sour sauce, sautéed abalone with chicken and asparagus, and fried pigeon eggs with walnuts. After dinner, they all went to the Li family's grand residence at No. 9 Great Sweetwater Well Street. Hsu Ying seemed more impressed by the spacious official residence than with her new boyfriend, perhaps because of her nervousness on their first date. The party lasted late into the evening. Those present talked about everything under the sun. Fang-Kuei even asked them to speak into his new wax cylinder recording machine, which he had brought back from Europe. When Hsu Ying was asked to say something into the machine, unbelievable as it may seem today, she didn't know what to say! In later years, Hsu Ying would become a gifted conversationalist never at a loss for words and a gracious host.

No. 9 Great Sweetwater Well Street was located in a bustling part of Peking east of the Forbidden Palace. There were four main courtyards with flower-decked gates, open halls, and trees of various sorts -- peach, plum, and pine. In one of the side courtyards, there was a sweetwater well, after which the street was named. There were many Taihu rock formations displayed throughout the courtyards as well as many studies (*shufang*) for young scholars to practice calligraphy and prepare for the examinations. There were altogether more than 80 rooms and halls. Many covered passageways wound through the gardens, which abounded in trees and flowering plants, including wisteria, crabapple, and lilacs. The front gate was painted bright red, with stone blocks along the side for mounting and dismounting horses. Inside the gate was a station for sedan chairs. The door sill, which was over a foot high, could be lifted out for horse drawn carriages, and later, rickshaws and cars to pass through. There was also a date tree on the sidewalk, which leaned over the street. This was the official residence built by Fang-Kuei's father, Li Guangyu, who personally supervised its construction. This magnificent mansion witnessed many ups and downs of Chinese history over the years.

When the dinner and the after-dinner party finally ended, Hsu Ying discovered that she had lost the yellow chrysanthemum that had been pinned to the lapel of her dark velvet overcoat. Three years later, however, it was unexpectedly recovered!

1930 Excursion to Guangdong, Guangxi and Hainan Island

After his return to China in November, Fang-Kuei spent roughly a year researching his prospective project. He traveled north to Peking from Shanghai, then back to Shanghai, and then further south to Guangdong, Guangxi, and the Hainan Island, where he spent a month traveling around listening to different dialects. On Hainan Island, he first followed the coast from Haikou to Lingao and then south to Lehui. In Fang-Kuei's own words:

I went there and began to listen to Chinese Hainan dialects of that area. It struck me that the so-called "b" and "d"s are not the same as the voiced ones. People always thought they were voiced b and d's, but I thought they were not. I thought they were implosive b and d's. Very similar, later I found out, to the Vietnamese "b" and "d"s and, also very similar to the Thai "b" and "d"s.

Hainan Island was difficult to reach during the 1930s, but with money from the Rockefeller Foundation, Fang-Kuei could afford to take a boat from Hong Kong to the port of Haikou. It was on this research trip that he devised an instrument for detecting the implosive nature of the consonants b and d.

. . . I borrowed some instruments from the Medical College of Canton University, and I made some very crude instruments out of a cigarette tin box. The tin box I put over my mouth, drilled a hole on the other side, with a rubber tubing connecting it to a so-called rubber tember, so if I blew with my breath through the tin can, the air would go through the tember. If you blow into it, the needle will go up; if it is implosive the needle will go down. So, in this way, I experimented with the Hainanese implosive consonants. . . (Li 1988: 31)

Fig. 12. Hainan Island where Li did preliminary field work, 1929-1930
(Courtesy of National Geographic)

Before ending this excursion, Li also traveled to Lingyun, Guangxi, to study the Yao language of that region. Subsequently, he reported the results of his findings to the Academia Sinica, which submitted them to the government.

1930 Officially Becomes a Research Fellow of the Academia Sinica

Following his research on Hainan dialects and the Yao language in Guangxi, Fang-Kuei became a full-fledged Research Fellow of the Academia Sinica, drawing a regular salary. He notified the Rockefeller Foundation that he no longer needed the fellowship. As a research fellow Fang-Kuei began his life-long devotion to the Institute of History and Philology and dedicated his life to the study of Chinese linguistics, focusing on minority languages and dialects.

1930 Publications

1930 saw the publication of three important works by Li Fang-Kuei:

1) *Mattole, an Athabaskan Language*. Chicago: University of Chicago Press. 152 pp.

This volume, his Ph.D. dissertation, was a landmark work because of its clear, concise, and accurate descriptive analysis of Mattole. It was also destined to become the only extant record of this language, since Fang-Kuei interviewed the last two Mattole Indians who spoke the language.

2) "A Study of Sarcee Verb-stems," *International Journal of American Linguistics (IJAL)* 6: 3-27.

This analysis, based on Sapir's field work was Li's first foray into American Indian linguistics. Much impressed by his student's work, Sapir promised to have it published. Both scholars must have been proud to see it appear in such a prestigious journal.

3) "Guangxi Lingyun Yao hua [The Yao Dialect of Lingyun]," *Bulletin of the Institute of History and Philology, Academia Sinica (BIHP)* 1.4: 419-426.

This piece, although short, was the first academic study of a minority language from southwest China. At the culmination of this pivotal year, Fang-Kuei already had a rough idea of the region he wanted to study.

1931 Spring Hsu Ying's Brother, Hsu Dau-lin, Returns to China

In the meanwhile, Fang-Kuei and Hsu Ying's relationship was hanging in the balance. The return of Hsu Ying's brother, Hsu Dau-lin, to China was a much awaited event, the reason being that Hsu Ying's mother did not have much faith in these young men who had studied abroad, dressed in foreign clothes, brought back foreign tastes, ideas, and manners. She had to wait until her son, Hsu Dau-lin, himself a returned student from Germany (he had been studying law at the University of Berlin), returned to China to pass judgment on Fang-Kuei. As luck would have it, Fang-Kuei, being a long-time student of German who had recently visited Berlin, impressed Dau-lin immediately. The two men instantly felt at home with each other, and approval was assured. However, Hsu Ying's mother still had her doubts. She asked her son:

"Your sister has been spoiled at home. The Li family is not well off. If they don't have enough money, how will your sister live?"

Dau-lin replied: "Fang-Kuei has a good position. Whether his family is wealthy or not does not really matter."

"What is this Academia Sinica? What kind of institution is it? I have never heard of it before. Will it last?"

"My goodness! The recently established Academia Sinica is the highest academic institution in the country. What is there to worry about? Since he has become its member, he has the qualifications to teach at any university in the country."

"Would any university want to hire someone to teach linguistics? What kind of study is it? I don't know what it's all about."

"You're not the only one who does not know! Lots of people don't know. It is a study about the way people talk."

"What! That's ridiculous! Except for a deaf-mute, who doesn't know how to talk? What is there to study? How many people are there who have nothing better to do than to study the way people talk?"

"Right! There are very few people in this field of study; it is a neglected field. Because there are few people, Fang-Kuei may become an authority in the field."

"Oh, in that case, he does have a future; and universities will hire him. But if the university terminates his contract, then what?" (Hsu Ying 2010: 50-51)

Exasperated, Dau-lin finally promised her: "If my little sister ever needs help, I will support her." This was exactly what his mother wanted to hear! Hsu Ying and Fang-Kuei were soon engaged to be married.

1931 Publication

"*Qieyun* â de laiyuan (The Sources of Ancient Chinese Vowel a)," *BIHP* 3.1:1-38。

This was Fang-Kuei's first article and a breakthrough in the study of archaic Chinese phonology. He sifted through the findings of more than half a dozen traditional Qing scholars who had worked on Chinese phonology, including Gu Yenwu, Duan Yucai, Jiang Yong, and others. And by selecting the most reliable data, he proposed that the *Qieyun* â, dating from the Tang dynasty (618-907), was derived from two vowels in archaic Chinese: a and e.

As Li had promised Fu Ssu-nien two years earlier that he would look into Chinese phonology, this 38-page article justified Fu's faith in Fang-Kuei. The importance of this study cannot be overstated: it was the first article on Chinese phonology in Chinese using scientific linguistic methodology.

1931 September 18 Mukden Incident: Japanese Invasion of China Begins

The Mukden (now Shenyang) Incident in Manchuria marked the official beginning of the Second Sino-Japanese War (1931-1945). By the 1930s Japan's designs on China had become more and more obvious. On September 18, 1931, the Japanese instigated the Mukden Incident as a pretext for bringing more troops into Manchuria. This incident was the initial step in Japanese militarist aggression in China: first taking control of Manchuria, next setting up the puppet state of Manchukuo, and then invading the rest of China.

The Academia Sinica, which had moved to Peking from Guangzhou, now had to move to Nanjing as the war clouds loomed on the horizon.

1932 August 21 Wedding of Fang-Kuei and Hsu Ying

After a three-year long courtship, Fang-Kuei and Hsu Ying were finally married in the Assembly Hall of North Sea Park in the center of Peking. There was a large entourage of friends, relatives, and distinguished guests in attendance. Dr. Hu Shih, a good friend of the family, and a distinguished scholar, activist and diplomat, was the Master of Ceremonies. After the ceremony, but before the wedding banquet,

Fig. 13. Hsu Ying at her wedding, 1932

Hsu Ying's mother-in-law, He Zhaoying, bowing deeply before the bewildered young bride said, "My home and my son are now yours. I hope you will care for them both to the best of your ability!" Hsu Ying was overwhelmed and terrified by this heavy responsibility suddenly thrust upon her. How could she be certain that she will be able to bear this responsibility?

The greatest surprise of the wedding day happened in the evening, when Fang-Kuei presented Hsu Ying with a dried chrysanthemum blossom, which he had carefully saved from their first date three years earlier. She thought she had lost it on their first date, but all this time Fang-Kuei had kept it safely hidden away!

1932 Publications

1) "Ancient Chinese *-ung, -uk, -uoug, -uok*, etc. in Archaic Chinese," *BIHP* 3.3:375–414.

This was Fang-Kuei's second article on Archaic Chinese phonology. Archaic Chinese was not his primary field of interest, but his research in the field always yielded fruitful results.

2) "A List of Chipewyan Stems," *IJAL* 7:122–151。

Even though he was now in China engaged in other research projects, he continued to work on his Chipewyan materials, which he had brought with him to China. Having completed a study of Chipewyan verb-stems, he submitted it for publication in the *International Journal of American Linguistics*

1932 Translation of Bernhard J. Karlgren's *Phonologie Chinoise*

In 1932 Fang-Kuei joined the collaborative efforts of Y.R. Chao (1892-1982) and Lo Ch'ang-p'ei (1899-1958), two of Li's more senior colleagues at the Institute in translating and updating Bernhard Karlgren's (1889-1978) magnum opus *Études sur la phonologie chinoise*. Karlgren's *Phonologie Chinoise*, written in French, was published in 1926. It was a monumental work of almost 900 pages, which took Karlgren 10 years to complete. Originally the *Phonologie* was Karlgren's doctoral dissertation, which he completed in 1915. But for the next ten years he continued his research on the subject and finally completed it in 1926. Karlgren went to China in 1910 when he was a young man of 21 and lived in Shanxi province for two years, from 1910 to 1912, gathering much valuable material.

In the summer of 1924 Y.R. Chao met Karlgren in Goteborg and suggested the translation of his *Phonologie*. At the time Karlgren wanted to revise his work, making it simpler and more readable. However, by 1931 Karlgren wrote Chao informing him that he had given up attempts to revise the work. Immediately, Chao and Lo began translating the book and together translated some 300-plus pages.

In 1932 the translation of the work became the joint project of the China Education and Culture Foundation and the Institute of History and Philology of the Academia Sinica, with the financial support of the former. The completed translation would be published by the Institute of the Academia Sinica.

It was at this point that Li Fang-Kuei joined the project. Parts I and II of the text had already been rendered into Chinese orally by Chao, who read his version into a recorder. Then Lo compared Chao's translation with the original French and transcribed it in Chinese. Portions of Part III (Chapters. 7–16), the historical part, were translated orally by Li and transcribed by Lo, and the remainder was translated by Li and Lo on their own. The whole of Part III was then edited by Lo. Part IV, consisting primarily of vocabulary, was transcribed into the international phonetic script by Yang Shifeng. Even though the three scholars were each responsible for different parts of the book, the finished product was a joint collaborative effort.

Finally, Y.R. Chao was responsible for reviewing the entire manuscript for accuracy and consistency. However, the reviewing process took its toll; Chao became exhausted and could not work on it anymore. At this point Ding Shengshu, another member of the Institute, stepped in to read over the entire manuscript and to check the accuracy of all the

Fig. 14. Bernhard B. Karlgren

references. Only then was the manuscript ready for publication. To reflect the appearance of new scholarship, Karlgren's work had to be constantly updated and revised. It was not just a simple mechanical translation.

1933 Publications

1) "Letter from Li Fang-Kuei," *BIHP Special Volume no.1*, 849–851。

Li's letter, addressed to Shen Jianshi, expresses his thoughts about the traditional scholarship on ancient texts. It was Mr. Shen who initially guided Fang-Kuei when he began his study of traditional works on Chinese phonology.

2) "Certain Phonetic Influences of the Tibetan Prefixes upon the Root Initials," *BIHP* 4.2.135–157。

Fang-Kuei started his research on Tibetan at this time. This was the first of a long series of his studies on Tibetan and Sino-Tibetan linguistics.

3) "Chipewyan Consonants," *BIHP Special Volume no. 1*, 429–467.

Li continued his work on Chipewyan. Instead of submitting this second article on Chipewyan for publication in America, Li decided to publish it in Academia Sinica's own *Bulletin of the Institute of History and Philology, Academia Sinica* (*BIHP*), in order to give it more international recognition.

1933 Summer: Fang-Kuei and Chinese Painting

In the summer of 1933, when Fang-Kuei was resting at home due to a slight indisposition, he felt the urge to do some painting. He asked for paper and paints and painted a series of 14 album-sized paintings of flowers, insects, and animals. His mother saw them and was very pleased, whereupon Hsu Ying immediately had them mounted and made into an album. This album was one of the few possessions the family treasured and took with them wherever they traveled, even during the war. The album was shown to a number of distinguished guests in the Li's home throughout the years, who were invited to leave a sample of their calligraphy in the album. In time this has become a valuable item of historical significance.

One year Fang-Kuei lent the album to his colleague at the University of Washington, Professor Irving Reifler, and forgot about it. Hsu Ying searched the house desperately for it, but could not find it. Then in 1962, after Professor Reifler passed away and his office was being cleaned out, his colleagues found this long-lost album and returned it to its rightful owner. Much relieved and gratified, Hsu Ying wrote, "It was a great joy to find something that has been lost for a long time!" The family album is now in the possession of Fang-Kuei's son, Peter.

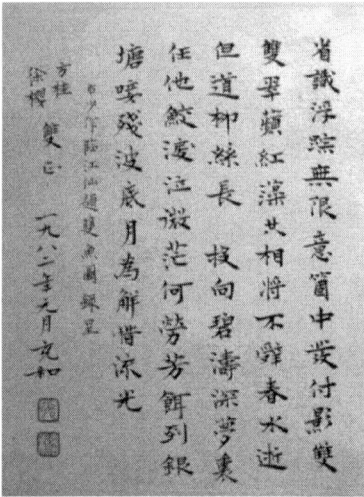

Fig. 15. A Leaf from Fang-Kuei's 1933 Album with Chang Ch'ung-ho's calligraphy

1933 May 17 Lindy is born

Fang-Kuei and Hsu Ying have their first child, a daughter, Lindy, born in the Red Cross Hospital in Shanghai, China. It was a difficult birth for Hsu Ying. Fortunately, Fang-Kuei's sister, Li Yi, was a pathologist at the hospital and helped make the conditions as comfortable as possible during the surgical procedure for the new mother. Because of Grandma He Zhaoying's wish for a grandson, she gave Lindy the nickname "*lingdi* (bring a little brother)". The name stuck, and she did actually bring a younger brother, 22 months later.

1933 Studies Siamese in Thailand

In order to better prepare himself to study the Tai languages of China's southwestern region, Fang-Kuei first decided to go to Thailand for three months' intensive study of Siamese (aka Thai, not the same as the Tai dialects in China). To this end he received approval and support from the Institute.

Because China had no diplomatic relations with Thailand in those days, it was not easy to get there. He had to go first to Singapore to get his visa and then take a train to Bangkok. While in Singapore, he met a Thai prince, Phya Damrong, who introduced him to some friends in Thailand. (Fig. 17) However, Fang-Kuei already had Chinese contacts in Thailand, who helped him rent a house at a reasonable rate

Fig. 16. Hsu Ying and daughter Lindy with grandmother,
He Zhaoying in Peking

Fig. 17. Li Fang-Kuei with officials in Singapore

when he arrived. Then he found two high school teachers-- one to teach him to read Thai and the other to practice conversation with him. He read up on the history of Thailand, against the advice of his teacher, who thought it might be too difficult for him, not realizing that Li was a gifted linguist who had studied many languages. After three months of intensive study, he gained a "thorough general knowledge of Thai."

1934 October 12: The Institute of History and Philology (IHP) Moves into Beijige in Nanjing

After the outbreak of the Sino-Japanese War in 1931, the IHP decided to move from Beijing to Shanghai, and then to Nanjing, joining the other institutes within Academia Sinica already established there. In October 1934 the Institute of History and Philology finally moved into its new building called the Beijige (North Pole Tower), close to the famous Buddhist temple, Jimingsi (Cock Crow Temple). Li had an office on the second floor across the hall from Y.R. Chao. Chao wrote about his neighbor, Li Fang-Kuei, across the hall, in an essay written in the 1970s,

It was in the Institute of History and Philology of Academia Sinica that I began to be closely associated with Li, at first in Peking, then in Nanking [now Nanjing], where my office in Peichi Ko [aka Beijige], was right across the hallway on the second floor. I had the pleasure of visiting in 1973 the same

Fig. 18. Beijige (North Star Tower) in the old days, 1934

Fig. 19. Beijige today

rooms in the same green-tiled-roof building, which is now occupied by a research institute in paleontology and related subjects. (Chao 1975)

1935 May 8–June 2: Field Work with Y.R. Chao in Jiangxi

Y.R. Chao, Li Fang-Kuei, and Yang Shifeng carried out field work on Jiangxi dialects for close to a month. They visited a several cities, including Jiujiang, Nanchang, Jian, Ganzhou. May 31 was the last day of their field work together. Chao and Li worked together on recording the Yongxin and Fengxin dialects.

1935–36: Field work in Guangxi with *Wuming* and *Longzhou* Dialects.

After studying Siamese intensively for three months during 1934–35, Fang-Kuei began his systematic study of Tai dialects in China spoken by the various minorities in Guangxi and other areas. In October 1935, he began his first extensive linguistic expedition to Guangxi, which lasted for four months (to February 1936). Because of the turmoil created by the Second Sino-Japanese War (1931–1945), it was not possible to go directly overland from Nanjing to Nanning, Guangxi.

Fang-Kuei had to take a train from Nanjing to Shanghai, then go by sea from Shanghai to Guangzhou, and finally by car from Guangzhou to Nanning, a distance of about 360 miles. Today you can drive that distance in eight hours. Once in Nanning, Fang-Kuei worked for a month with Mr. Su

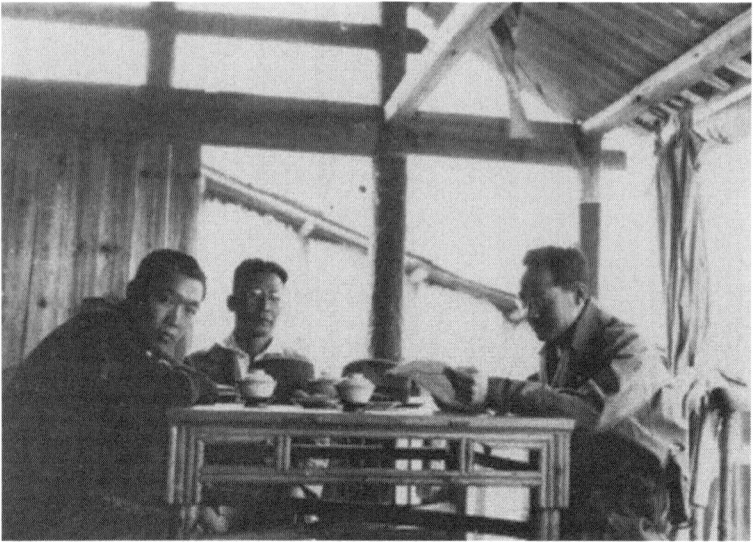

Fig. 20. R to L, Y.R. Chao, Li Fang-Kuei and
Yang Shifeng

Fig. 21. Fang-Kuei with the Su family in Matoucun

Zengwei, on the Wuming dialect. Su was a native of Matoucun, a village just north of the town of Wuming, about 50 miles north of Nanning. Mr. Su was an excellent informant who sang folk songs and told stories. In all, Li collected 12 stories, some 14 folk songs, and songs about daily activities.

Later, Su Zengwei accompanied Li and his assistant, Mr. Wu Zongji, to Matoucun to gather more materials. Even though the distance from Nanning to Wuming was only about 60 miles, which can be driven in about an hour today, Li's group traveled on foot for over two days and had to climb across the Daming Mountains in order to reach Matoucun. Furthermore, they brought heavy recording instruments with them (they had to hire a bearer to carry the equipment), which further slowed the journey. Since there were no hotels in Matoucun, Li lived with his informant, Mr. Su, and his family, while doing his research. Li snapped this photo with the Su family in their home (Fig. 21).

After studying Wuming, Fang-Kuei worked with two other informants, Ms. Li Ping and Mr. Feng Weihan on the Longzhou dialect. Longzhou was about 160 miles southwest of Nanning. Today that distance could be covered in about four hours. Li worked with these two informants for a month, recording 12 stories, narratives on marriage customs, funeral ceremonies, and a song on the famous story of star-crossed lovers Liang Shanbo and Zhu Yingtai. Li's analysis of the Longzhou dialect was published in 1940 and received the

Fig. 22. Field Work in Nanning, Wuming, Longzhou,
Guangxi, 1934–1935 (Courtesy of National Geographic)

Yang Quan Prize from the Academia Sinica for scholarly excellence. After working on Wuming and Longzhou, Li and his assistant, Wu Zongji, journeyed up the You River to northwest Guangxi to study Tai dialects in the area of Tianbao, Xilin, Bose (about 200 miles from Naning), Lingyun, Qianjiang, etc. During these four months, Fang-Kuei studied altogether over 20 dialects in the region.

1935 February 24: Peter is born

Fang-Kuei and Hsu Ying's second child, Peter, was born in the Central Hospital in Nanjing, China. After waiting nine anxious months, Hsu Ying was relieved that the second child was a boy. Fang-Kuei's mother had been clamoring for a boy ever since Lindy was born. Now she was satisfied and Lindy's mission was fulfilled.

1936 Publication: "Language and Dialects"

"Languages and Dialects," *The China Year Book (1935)*, 121–128。

This was an important article because it was the first publication to give a comprehensive description of the languages and dialects of China. According to Professor Anne Yue, Li was the first linguist to formulate the phonological criteria for classifying Chinese dialects into eight major groups: 1) Northern Mandarin, 2) Eastern Mandarin, 3) Southwestern Mandarin, 4) Wu, 5) Gan-Hakka, 6) Min, 7) Yue, and 8) Xiang.

1937 First Home in Nanjing at 19 Tianmu Road

In 1937, Fang-Kuei and Hsu Ying designed their own house at 19 Tianmu Road in Nanjing. It was a two-story brick house with four bedrooms and two living rooms. The house was of modest size with a big yard. The kitchen and bathrooms were designed to function according to the family's needs. The garden and pavilions were elegantly laid out. After the house was completed, the family moved in but lived in it for only three months because Fang-Kuei received an invitation to teach at Yale University in the fall of 1937. Even though the family returned to China two years later, in 1939, the outbreak of the Sino-Japanese War prevented them from returning to their home in Nanjing.

In the meantime, the Academia Sinica had also moved from Nanjing to Kunming, Yunnan province, by this time. Therefore, the Li family moved inland, to Longtou Village, in the northern suburb of Kunming. Eventually, after the end of the war, the family moved back into their home in Nanjing in 1946. But, as fate would have it, they were about to be uprooted again: Fang-Kuei received an invitation from Harvard University as a visiting professor to teach and participate in compiling a dictionary. Therefore, they stayed in

Fig. 23. 19 Tianmu Road as it looks today, 2014. The old house was replaced with a huge apartment complex.

the house for barely three months before they had to leave for America. This time they were gone for more than thirty years!

In the fall of 1978 Hsu Ying and Fang-Kuei visited China for the first time after 32 years. They returned to their first home in Nanjing, during a lull between Fang-Kuei's lectures and visits to old friends and relatives. When Hsu Ying knocked at the door of their former home, a polite couple opened it and invited them in. This couple had been living in the house for over 20 years, whereas the real owners, Fang-Kuei and Hsu Ying, lived there for a total of only six months! Hsu Ying reflected philosophically: "In this topsy-turvy world, we are all travelers, who come and go. Who is the tenant and who is the owner, who is to say, who is to say?"

Some 36 years later, on January 9, 2014, the owners' son, Peter and his wife, Marjorie, visited 19 Tianmu Road; and this is what the place looks like today (Fig. 23). Our old house was torn down and replaced by a large apartment complex with some 300 units. Tianmu Road is still a relatively quiet street compared to the busy Beijing West Road running parallel to it one block north.

1937 March 19 Fang-Kuei Receives Letter from Edward Sapir

It must have been a great pleasure for Li Fang-Kuei to receive a letter from his former teacher at the University of Chicago, Edward Sapir, who was now teaching at Yale University, inviting him to teach at Yale as a visiting professor for a three-year term.

Sapir and Fang-Kuei had developed a close relationship during their time at Chicago. In fact, Sapir had hoped Li would stay in America to continue the study of American Indian languages; but Li made up his mind to return to China. During the ten years from 1928 to 1937 Sapir had not forgotten his brilliant student. In the meantime, Sapir had moved to Yale University in 1931 and wanted his former student to join him there.

On March 25th of the same year, Franklin Edgerton, Professor of Sanskrit and Chair of the Department of Oriental Studies at Yale University, wrote a long and detailed letter to Fang-Kuei, formally inviting him to teach at Yale as Visiting Professor of Chinese Linguistics for a three-year period, from July 1, 1937, to June 30, 1940, at an annual salary of $5,000.00. The letter also mentioned that Edward Sapir would be visiting China in the same year. However, that was not to be because Sapir suffered a severe heart attack and had to be hospitalized.

1937 July 7: Marco Polo Bridge Incident

The Marco Polo Bridge Incident of 1937, which took place outside Peking, marked the beginning of China's all-out War of Resistance against Japan, which lasted for 8 bloody years, from 1937 to 1945. The Marco Polo Bridge Incident marked the second time (the first was the Mukden Incident of 1931) that the Japanese instigated such an event as an excuse for moving their troops into Peking. In the years between the two incidents, Japan consolidated her hold in Manchuria and was ready to invade China proper, beginning with Peking.

During the 14 years from 1931 to 1945, more than 30 million Chinese people (including civilians) were killed, and 90 million more were dislocated from their homes. These refugees had to flee from one part of the country to another; many factories and institutions, including the Academia Sinica, had to move from Nanjing via Kunming and then to Lizhuang, an out-of-the-way town in southwestern Sichuan.

1937 July 17: Narrow Escape from Nanjing

After receiving the letter of invitation to teach at Yale, Fang-Kuei requested a leave of absence from the Academia Sinica for three years. But he was only granted a two-year leave of absence. The Li family, who had just moved into their new house on Tianmu Road in Nanjing, now had to leave it behind.

To be sure that he had the necessary materials for his teaching assignment, Fang-Kuei decided to take his books to Shanghai first and then to return to Nanjing to get the family. However, as soon as he arrived in Shanghai, the Shanghai-Nanjing trains ceased to run on a regular schedule because of Japanese air raids. Fang-Kuei was stuck and cut off in Shanghai.

Meanwhile, Hsu Ying had to find some way to reach Shanghai on her own with her two young children: Peter, age two and Lindy, four. At the same time, she also had to look after two elder parents, her own mother and her mother-in-law, both of whom had come all the way from Peking to see the family off to America. Faced with a serious dilemma, Hsu Ying sought advice from their good family friend and Fang-Kuei's senior colleague Dr. Hu Shih (who had been the master of ceremonies at their wedding). Hsu Ying wrote:

As soon as Mr. Hu saw me, he cried out, "Aiya! How come you are still here? What are you waiting for?" Then I told him about my problem: firstly, my two mothers from Peking were in town. Who will take care of them? Secondly, with the war worsening, should we be going to the United States at all? Dr. Hu always said that he was a diehard optimist. In spite of the seriousness of the situation, he said light-heartedly, "What can Fang-Kuei do about the family problem? You have your brothers here. Secondly, what can Fang-Kuei do about the war? He is not going to carry a rifle and go into battle! Under the present circumstances, it is better that he go overseas. Knowledge knows no national boundaries; the sooner he can contribute to the growth of knowledge, the better off we will be. Don't hesitate any more, leave immediately, leave immediately (kuaizou, kuaizou)!. . . .

The real problem is how to get you and the two children to Shanghai safely in case there should be strafing and bombing along the way. Let me think, let me think. I have it! Mr. Zhang Weici, the deputy director of the Railroad Department, is here in Nanjing by himself while his family is in Shanghai. Let's find out when he is returning to Shanghai. Since he is by himself, he could help you look after the children." (Hsu Ying 2010:62–63)

After the arrangements were made with Mr. Zhang, Hsu Ying had another request. In spite of the war, Hsu Ying insisted on celebrating her mother-in-law's 60th birthday before leaving for Shanghai. After Dr. Hu heard her out, he remarked, "Young Lady [he said in English], you are certainly full of ideas! Do you realize how serious the situation is, and you still want to have a birthday party for your mother? . . . Well, all right, considering the fact that we all love our mothers, I'll fulfill your wish and arrange a birthday party for her!"

The day after the birthday party, Hsu Ying bade goodbye to the two mothers and left quickly for the railway station with Deputy Director Zhang. The air-raid sirens began to sound as they boarded the train. Ordinarily the ride from Nanjing to Shanghai took about 3 hours, but this time it took a full 24 hours. The train had to make many stops along the way. On the night of July 17th, the moon was especially bright, making the train a perfect target for Japanese planes. When the Japanese planes approached, the train had to stop, and the passengers were told to leave the train and hide in the fields until the planes were gone. Who would get back on the train and who would not was a matter of fate.

Finally, on the evening of the 18th there was a tearful but happy family reunion at the train station in Shanghai. However, the family had to wait another two weeks before boarding the USS Hoover and sailing for the United States in September, 1937. Three months later there occurred the horrific Nanjing Massacre, in which over 300,000 people were killed in the most brutal fashion imaginable during a six week period. The Li family was indeed fortunate to have escaped earlier.

Fig. 24. Passport photo of the Li family, 1937.

Fig. 25. The Li Family on board the USS Hoover,
Sailing for America, 1937.

Chapter IV.

Interim: Two Years at Yale
Second Trip to America
1937-1939

Interim: Two Years at Yale
1937-1939

1937 October 7 Arrival in New Haven

Fang-Kuei and family arrived in New Haven on October 7, 1937. The university arranged housing for them at 134 Hubinger St. in New Haven. Professor George Kennedy met them at the train station and took them to their new home, where they were to live for the next 18 months. Professor Kennedy also arranged a car for Fang-Kuei to drive.

Two weeks after their arrival at Yale, Fang-Kuei developed severe abdominal pain. Hsu Ying tried to help by massaging his abdomen, which was great mistake. The pain turned out to be from appendicitis. Hsu Ying's massage could have ruptured the appendix. Fang-Kuei was taken to the emergency room the next morning and had an appendectomy. After her husband's operation and recuperation, Hsu Ying decided that she had to learn how to drive in case there was another emergency.

On a warm, sunny day, after packing the whole family into the car (another mistake), Hsu Ying took the wheel with Fang-Kuei as coach. She drove down the street smoothly and made a left turn, but she did not let go of the steering wheel after

Fig. 26. The Li family at 134 Hubinger St, New Haven, Connecticut

making the turn. The car crashed into a tree. The children, Peter and Lindy, tumbled onto the floor but were unhurt. Hsu Ying was not hurt, but Fang-Kuei soon felt his hand swell inside his glove. He had stubbed his thumb and had to make another trip to the emergency room.

After this accident, Hsu Ying decided not to pursue her driving lessons anymore. However, when Franklin Edgerton, professor of Sanskrit at Yale, heard about this, he insisted that Hsu Ying continue to learn. He said, "If you stop now, you will always be afraid to drive." He took it upon himself to coach Hsu Ying. In those days, driving schools were not that common. After three or four lessons, he said, "Now you can practice on your own." But she never did. It was not until some ten years later, on her second trip to the States, in 1947, that she learned to drive.

1937 Fang-Kuei Teaches Chinese Phonology

While at Yale Fang-Kuei taught only one course on Chinese Phonology while continuing with his research projects. There were not many students interested in Chinese phonology at that time. Fang-Kuei's students were mostly faculty members at Yale University. However, there were two special students from Harvard: Professors Sergei Elisseef (1889–1975), Director of the Harvard-Yenching Institute, and James R. Ware, professor of Chinese at Harvard. The two of them took the train every week from Boston to New Haven to attend Li's class.

1937 Fang-Kuei Visits Sapir at New York Hospital

Following his arrival at Yale, Fang-Kuei was saddened to learn that his professor and mentor, Edward Sapir (1884– 1939), was not on campus that year. Sapir had had a stroke and had become seriously ill. Li went to the hospital in New York to visit him, bringing the family with him. Sapir was very pleased to see Fang-Kuei, since he was one of Sapir's favorite students. During the ten years since Li's departure from Chicago, Sapir had not forgotten him. It was he who had written to Fang-Kuei at the Academia Sinica in Nanjing, inviting him to teach at Yale. Fang-Kuei visited him three or four times in New York before he passed away.

1938 A Star Pupil in Hsu Ying's Painting Class

While in New Haven, Hsu Ying registered for a course on watercolor painting at Larson College. Sometimes Fang-Kuei would tag along, since he had to drive Hsu Ying to class. Often he would also sketch and paint with the other students. One day, out of curiosity, the teacher, Ms. Beverly Smith, asked if she may see his painting. As soon as she saw his work, she was amazed. His work was by far the best in the class. From then on he became the star student even though he was not registered for the class. Of course, she did not know that Fang-Kuei was an accomplished painter in the Chinese traditional style.

Fig. 27. A watercolor painting by Fang-Kuei
while in New Haven, c. 1938.

1938 A *Kunqu* Benefit Performance for the War Effort

As the War of Resistance against Japan raged on in China, the students and faculty at Yale and the overseas Chinese community at large felt it was their patriotic duty to help in the war effort. With an abundance of artistic talent at Yale, the group decided to put on a cultural program to raise funds. One number in the program took the form of a scene, *Xiaoyan* (Small Banquet), from the famous *kun* opera *The Palace of Eternal Youth*. Since Hsu Ying was known for her singing of *kunqu*, she sang the lead role of Yang Guifei, working with Yao Xinnong, a playwright and student in the drama department, and a student in the music department who was studying flute. The story tells of the tragic love between the aging Tang Emperor Minghuang and his beautiful concubine, Yang Guifei. Because he was so enchanted with her, the emperor neglected to hold court with his ministers, which eventually cost him his empire.

So that the flutist would be able to play the music on a Western flute (different from the traditional Chinese bamboo flute), Fang-Kuei transcribed the music from the traditional Chinese score to the Western system of notation. It should be noted that the wife of the President of Yale University, Gladys Miriam Seymour, visited Hsu Ying to offer words of encouragement. Ms. Seymour suggested that formal dress should be worn on the night of the performance. Accordingly, all the men arrived in tuxedos and the ladies in evening gowns. The program was a smashing success. The highlight of the program was Hsu Ying's performance of the *kun* opera scene. The benefit performance raised more than $3,000, a sizable amount in those days. This was the first formal performance of a *kun* opera in the United States, according to Hsu Ying.

1939 February 4 The Passing of Edward Sapir

The passing of Edward Sapir was a great loss to the linguistic community. It was a greater loss for Fang-Kuei, who had studied with Sapir for three years--from the first moment he arrived in Chicago in 1926 until he left in 1929. Sapir was 42 at the time and had arrived at Chicago in 1925, a year before his young protégé enrolled there. Before accepting the professorship at Chicago, Sapir had served in the Geological Survey of Canada for 15 years as the in-house anthropologist. Apparently Sapir and Li hit it off very well. According to Fang-Kuei, Sapir liked him very much, and the two often chatted about many linguistic issues after class.

When Fang-Kuei left the United States to return to China in 1929, Sapir obtained a Rockefeller Foundation Fellowship for him either to do research in China or to return to America to continue his American Indian research, which Sapir hoped Fang-Kuei would do. Sapir also wanted to visit China in 1937, but his heart-attack prevented him from doing so. Sapir passed away on February 4, 1939, at the age of fifty-five, never having fulfilled his wish of going to China.

1939 The Family Returns to China

After an idyllic sojourn of 18 months in New Haven, the Li family had to leave their temporary haven and return to war-torn China. On the eve of their departure, there was an argument: Hsu Ying did not want to return to China with the children since China was at war. She wanted to take the children to Italy to join her brother, Hsu Dau-lin, who was a Cultural Attache. She thought it would be safer there than in China, not realizing that Europe would soon be embroiled in greater turmoil than China. For his part Fang-Kuei had promised to return to Academia Sinica after his two-year leave of absence.

Their disagreement was not resolved until the last moment, when they arrived at the travel agency. Fang-Kuei told the travel agent, "Three tickets for Italy and one for China." At that critical moment, Hsu Ying stepped forward and told the agent, "Wait, make that four to China, please!" For the next 7 years, during the war, the family moved from place to place a few paces ahead of the advancing Japanese troops in China's remote interior provinces.

1939 June Cross-Country Drive from New Haven to San Francisco

Having resolved the dispute, Fang-Kuei and family spent a leisurely month driving cross-continent from New Haven to San Francisco with stops at Mt. Rushmore, Yellowstone National

Park, Grand Canyon, and the Great Salt Lake; then on to Los Angeles and up the coast to San Francisco. They attended two World's Fairs, one in New York, the other in San Francisco. In New York, Hsu Ying and Fang-Kuei took their first roller coaster ride with their good friends Wei Jufeng and his wife. They were scared out of their wits. In San Francisco, they boarded their ship bound for China with a stop in Hawaii.

1939 July 6 Nine-Day Holiday in Honolulu

On July 6 the Li family arrived in Honolulu and stayed with Y.R. Chao and his family for nine days, enjoying the sunny beaches of Waikiki. A week later, on July 14 at 10 AM, the Lis boarded the Empress of Canada, heading east for China. At 10:00 PM on the same day, the Chao family set sail in the opposite direction on the USS Cleveland, bound for America. When the Chao family arrived in San Francisco, they drove the car Fang-Kuei left for them in San Francisco to New Haven, where Y.R. Chao would complete the remaining year of Li's teaching contract at Yale. This arrangement allowed Li to keep his promise to Fu Ssu-nien to return to China after a two-year leave of absence.

Fig. 28. The Li and Chao families in Honolulu, Hawaii. July, 1939.
Back row (L to R): Iris, Y.R.,?, Fang-Kuei, Nova; Front: Xiaozhong,
Lancy, Lindy, Peter (leaning on Hsu Ying), Mrs. Chao, Hsu Ying,

Chapter V.

Most Productive Years (II)

1939-1946

Most Productive Period (II): 1939-1946

1939 September Arrival in Kunming

When Fang-Kuei and his family returned to China in late summer 1939, the Academia Sinica was no longer in Nanjing. It had already moved to Kunming in China's southwest interior, far from the advancing Japanese forces. The Academia Sinica had to be several steps ahead of the Japanese in order to prevent its recently unearthed archeological treasures, valuable rare books, and rich trove of research materials from falling into Japanese hands. It first moved to Wuhan, but since Wuhan was a large industrial center, it soon became another target of attack for the Japanese. The Academia Sinica, therefore, had to move further inland to Kunming.

Since Shanghai and Nanjing were both under Japanese occupation, Fang-Kuei and family stayed only for a short time in the International Concessions in Shanghai. Then they embarked on a circuitous route to Kunming: sailing to Hong Kong, then to Haiphong in Vietnam, and from Haiphong by train to their ultimate destination, Kunming. When the family finally arrived, Fu Ssu-nien, Director of the Institute of History and Philology (IHP), was on hand to greet them. After all, Fang-Kuei was making good his promise to return after the two years' leave of absence even though the War of Resistance against Japan was raging at the time. He could have stayed on in America for the duration of the war, thus avoiding all the hardships of that bloody conflict.

But as it turned out, even Kunming was not safe from Japanese attacks. On September 23, 1938, the Japanese began bombing Kunming. Again, after nine months in Kunming, the Academia Sinica, together with a number of other universities and research institutions, moved their facilities to a northern suburb, a village called *Longtoucun* (Dragon Head Village).

1940 Kunming Becomes a Wartime Cultural Center

Even in the best of times, Kunming was not an easily accessible place, to say nothing about in times of war. But within a few years after the outbreak of all-out war with Japan in 1937, students, teachers, writers, musicians from all over China -- Peking, Shanghai, Tianjin, Nanjing, Wuhan -- flocked to Kunming, making it the new cultural and intellectual center of China. Many students and professors came on foot, walking hundreds of miles; others came by train, bus, truck, and the more fortunate by car. Many academic institutions, like the Academia Sinica, Peking University, Qinghua, Yanjing, Tongji, and others also moved their facilities there.

`Famous writers like Zhu Ziqing, Wen Yiduo, Lao She; historians Gu Jiegang, Wu Han, Liang Siyong; academic scholars

Li Chi, Liang Sicheng and his famous wife and socialite Lin Huiyin, Fu Ssu-nien, Li Fang-Kuei, Lo Ch'ang-p'ei, Wang Li, and many others all gathered in Kunming.

1939 Fang-Kuei's New House in Longtoucun

After arriving in Kunming, Fang-Kuei built a five-room house on a piece of land leased, with the aid of the Academia Sinica, from Mr. Zhang Yinong, a wealthy and educated landowner in Longtoucun. The reason the Lis needed five rooms was because both Fang-Kuei's mother and his mother-in-law came to Kunming to be with him. According to the contract, after four years, the house and land would revert back to Mr. Zhang.

The following is a passage from Zhang Yinong's autobiography:

In 1939, the Japanese invaders became more and more vicious. The Japanese-occupied territory grew larger and larger. The Academia Sinica withdrew to Xiangyingsi [Reciprocity Temple] in our village. Some of the people [attached to the Academia] rented houses, others built their own. On our empty lot, Li Fang-Kuei built a five-room house. The contract was for four years, after which the land and house would be unconditionally surrendered.

My sister, Lindy Li Mark, went back to Kunming in 2004 and wrote about her visit to "our" old house in Longtoucun:

The family that owned the land at that time, has now built a concrete block house bucked up against one side of "our" house. Our house, unlike the local architecture, had an open

plan with four main rooms in a row on a raised foundation. A veranda runs along the front, and semi-circular steps lead down to the yard. A separate building stands to the right, with a small chamber that used to be our chicken house. There was another small house to the left for my paternal grandmother, but that must have been taken out when the concrete house was built. The present owner, a granddaughter of the original owner, now uses "our house" as a granary and storage for farm implements. A memorial altar honoring her grandfather stands in what was our living room. This man kept a diary recording the lease of the land to my father. Is this really "our house"? It seems so much smaller than in my memory. Our house was one of two houses that had a fireplace, new fangled "wall hearths" that my American-educated father designed. So I looked for the fireplace, but found no trace of it. Later it turned out that the owners ripped it out because a cold draft was coming down the chimney. Moreover, they didn't know what to use it for. The house is still pretty solid; but the view of the rice fields and rolling hills is now cut off by a wall and iron doors to create a courtyard effect. We had an open bamboo lattice fence there."
(Mark, L. L, "Christmas Newsletter," 2004)

Fig 29. The front steps of "our" house in Longtoucun

圖十五：昆明龍頭村李方桂先生舊居

Fig. 30. Fang-Kuei's house in Longtoucun, Kunming today, 2004.

1939 Autumn Studies on the Bo'ai (aka Po-Ai)

After his return to China in the fall of 1939, without skipping a beat, Li Fang-Kuei immediately spent two months focusing on the Boai dialect, taking advantage of the fact that an informant, Mr. Guan Dengshi, had come to Longtoucun to study. He spoke a northern dialect of the Tai language. According Fang-Kuei, he was an excellent informant. Mr. Guan not only had clear pronunciation, he was also a good storyteller. He spoke slowly and fluently, and his delivery was lively. Therefore, in just two months, Fang-Kuei recorded an abundance of materials: 24 songs and 8 riddles. The vocabulary was especially rich. A number of young scholars-- Chang Kun (aka Zhang Kun), Ma Xueliang, and Yang Shifeng--also participated in the project, making it particularly fruitful.

The study was published posthumously, in 1988-1990. Before his passing, Fang-Kuei wrote a prefatory note, thanking the following individuals for preparing the work for publication: Chang Kun for preparing the entire glossary, Yang Shifeng for recopying all the materials, and Gong Hwang-cherng for coordinating the final stages of publication.

1939 October Afternoon Tea in Longtoucun

It was not very often that children and adults gathered together to welcome a foreign visitor from afar. Sometime

Fig 31. Afternoon tea with a special guest Mrs. Yu (L6), Longtoucun, Kunming, October 1939. (L to R) L2 Fu Ssu-nien, L3 Lindy (leaning against Hsu Ying), L4 Hsu Ying, L5 Yu Ronghua (sitting on armrest), L 6 Mrs. Yu, L7 Jack Fu, L8 Dora Fu, Peter (leaning against Dora Fu), L9-10 unknown, L11 Fang-Kuei Li

in October 1939, Mrs. Yu from Chongqing came to visit her friends in Longtoucun. This was a special occasion for everyone to welcome the guest and her young daughter Yu Ronghua, the little girl with pigtails sitting beside her mother (Fig.31).

1939: Field work in Yunnan with the Sani Language

In the winter of 1939, after working with the Boai language, Li took his new assistant, Ma Xueliang, a recent graduate of Peking University, to a small village near Lunan called Weize to record the Sani language of the Yi minority group. Conditions there were especially harsh. The Yi people did not have many vegetables, and salt was in short supply. Meals for Li and Ma consisted of rice with dried beans and peppers.

During their field work, Li and Ma stayed with a Sani family. They were given a room in the attic located above the kitchen and storage area. The height of the room was less than that of an average person, so that they could not stand upright. Once they entered, they had to lie down on the floor. While the Sani family was cooking downstairs, the smoke from the stove seeped through the floor boards and filled their room. Ma observed that Li was so fully absorbed in his work that he was totally oblivious to the smoke and other discomforts of his surroundings. He continued to train and instruct his student in field work methods as if this was nothing out of the ordinary.

Fig. 32. A stern Li Fang-Kuei in Kunming, 1939
(Courtesy of IHP, Academia Sinica)

The harsh living conditions did not prevent Li from establishing good working relations with the locals, which made their field work easier. After a month of fieldwork, student and teacher had each lost about 15 lbs.

One of the unexpected discoveries made by the researchers was an interesting courtship custom among the Sani. Every night, Li noticed that his host would make his sixteen-year-old daughter leave the house. He learned there was a communal house where the young people gathered each night to sing and dance, trying to find a prospective mate. Li asked one of the locals to sneak him into the communal house so that he could see what was going on. He and Ma spent an exciting evening concealed in a dark corner observing the young people's cheerful singing and dancing around an indoor fire. After returning to Kunming, Li arranged to have a Sani informant in Kunming work further with Ma to complete his research project. Eventually, after accumulating forty to fifty stories, Ma completed his master's thesis and in 1941 received his degree. Later his study of the Sani Yi language became a landmark work in the application of modern methods in the study of minority languages.

Fig. 33. Ma Xueliang, Fang-Kuei's assistant, as a young man, ca.1940

1939 December 2 A Landmark Lecture on Sino-Tibetan Studies

Shortly after his return to China, Fang-Kuei gave an important public lecture at the Humanities Research Institute of Beijing University in Kunming. The title of the lecture was "Methodology on the Study of Sino-Tibetan Languages." Ma Xueliang, who attended the lecture, believed that it was an epoch-making lecture because of its comprehensive discussion of general linguistic issues, beginning with Indo-European developments and ending with approaches to Sino-Tibetan linguistics. Li's discussion of word classes, grammar, and genetic relationship between languages gave the audience new perspectives on approaches to Sino-Tibetan linguistics transcending the Indo-European model.

The lecture was enthusiastically received, and handwritten copies circulated widely. It was not officially published until March 1951, more than 10 years later. Since then it has been reprinted several times, most recently in 2014.

1939 A Birthday Party in Longtoucun, Kunming

In spite of the exigencies of war, a birthday party was still a birthday party, especially when two grandmothers were involved. The occasion was the birthday of Hsu Ying's mother, who was celebrating her 60th birthday. On this special occasion, many family members of the Institute of History and

Fig 34. A rare group photo of a birthday celebration, 1939.
Back row (L to R): Qian Duansheng, Li Fang-Kuei, unknown,
Xiao Lunhui; unknown, Mrs. Fu Ssu-nien, Mrs. Li Chi, Hsu
Ying, unknown, unknown, Mrs. Xiao Lunhui, Mr. Dong Zuobin,
Xiao Xin. Seated: Hsu Ying's mother and Fang-Kuei's mother.
Front row: L2 Dong Min, L4 Liang Boyou, L5 Lindy, L6 Peter,
L7 Li Guangmo (kneeling), L8 Jack Fu, L9 Xiao Xiaomei.

Philology, together with their children, gathered for this rare group photo (Fig. 34). There were 24 people altogether in the photo: eight wives, four husbands, ten children, and the two honored grandmothers, Hsu Ying and Fang-Kuei's mother.

1940 Fang-Kuei Turns Down an Administrative Position

When the Academia Sinica planned to establish an Institute of Anthropology, the Director of the IHP, Fu Ssu-nien, very much wanted Fang-Kuei to head the institute. He repeatedly tried to persuade Li to accept the position because of his international reputation. But Fang-Kuei had no intention of accepting the post. Finally, Fang-Kuei had to put those expectations to rest by answering bluntly, in no uncertain terms: "I believe, first-rate scholars are researchers, second-rate scholars are teachers, and third-rate scholars are administrators and officials!" Fu Ssu-nien replied, "Thank you. I am a third-rate scholar," and left disappointed.

Fu Ssu-nien must have felt hurt, but being the generous and broadminded scholar that he was, he did not hold it against Fang-Kuei. Fang-Kuei, for his part, being a person of uncompromising integrity and exceptional linguistic ability, probably would have been a poor administrator, given his lack of interest in bureaucratic and personnel details. But the fact that he was able to hurl such an insult and get away with it speaks volumes for Fu Ssu-nien's graciousness and generosity.

Throughout the years, the two men and their families have remained close.

1940 August Xing Gongwan joins the IHP

After graduating from Anhui University in 1937, Xing Gongwan passed the qualifying examinations for graduate studies at the Institute of History and Philology. But due to the circumstances of war he was not able to join the Institute until 1940. He wrote to Li asking for permission to register even though he was three years late. Li encouraged him to come and register and subsequently Xing became a graduate assistant and one of Li's devoted disciples. For the following two years, he took part in several of Fang-Kuei's field trips in Guizhou, visiting various minority groups.

1940 **Publication**

1) *Longzhou tuyu (The Tai Dialect of Lungchow: Text, Translations, and Glossary)*. *BIHP Special Vol. #16*. 290 pp.

Fang-Kuei's work on the Tai Dialect of Longzhou won him the coveted Yang Quan Award for outstanding field work and scholarship. The field work was done during 1935-1936.

2) Chao, Yuan-Ren., Lo Ch'ang-p'ei, and Li Fang-Kuei, trans. *Zhongguo yinyunxue yanjiu* (Studies in Chinese Phonology). Chinese translation of Bernhard Karlgren's ***Études sur la phonologie chinoise***. Peking: Commercial Press.

Fig. 35. Xing Gongwan, one of Fang-Kuei's
graduate assistants

The war time publication of the translation of Karlgren's monumental *Études sur la phonologie chinoise* by three of the most outstanding Chinese linguists, Chao, Lo, and Li, was a remarkable undertaking. There were often shortages of paper; the print plates were often damaged or destroyed due to the moves; and there was the need for special typefaces. It became the bible for linguists and graduate students of linguistics as soon as it was published.

1940 August The Academia Sinica Moves from Kunming to Lizhuang

In August 1940, the Nationalist government gave orders for the Academia Sinica to move to a safer location to protect its treasures from Japanese air raids. The anthropologist Rui Yifu was sent to find a suitable location. He declared the town of Lizhuang on the north bank of the Yangzi River near Yibin in southern Sichuan province to be the most suitable site. It was not even on any official maps.

By today's means of transportation, the distance from Kunming to Lizhung is about 360 miles and would take about a day to reach. But during the war in those days, there were no highways, and the roads were poor. Travelers had to go from Kunming to Qujing, then to Xuanwei, Weining, Bijie, Xuyong, Luzhou, Yibin, Nanxi, and finally Lizhuang (see Fig. 36). By this circuitous route the distance was close to 500 miles, and the trip usually took about two weeks if there were no unusual delays.

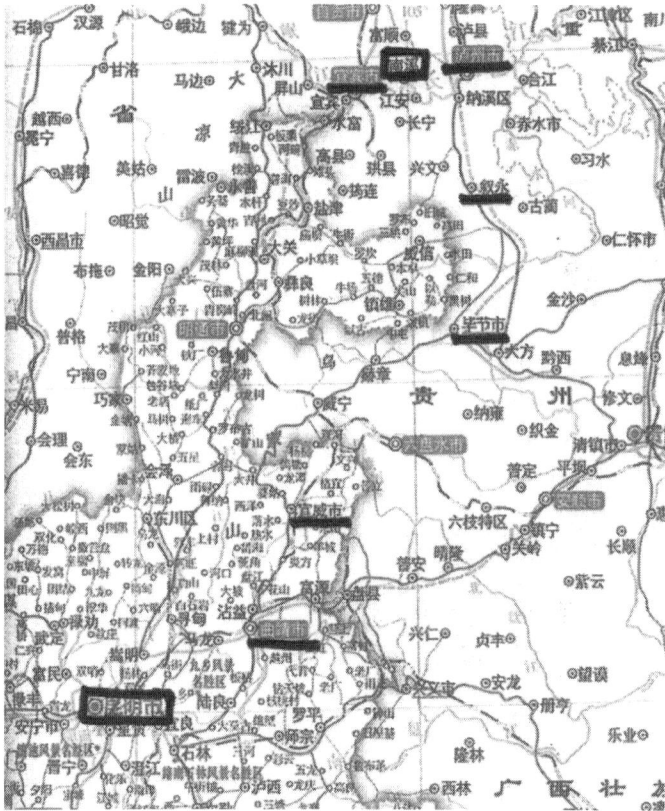

Fig 36. The circuitous route from Kunming to Lizhuang.
(From bottom to top Kunming and Nanxi in boxes)

Beginning in November 1940 the Academia Sinica and some other institutions began their slow and tortuous move to Lizhuang. There were often mishaps along the way. On November 12, the Institute of History and Philology's 140 crates of books fell into the river when they were being transferred onto to a ferry boat in Luzhou. Fortunately, the crates were quickly retrieved, and the damage was limited. But the water-soaked books had to be aired out and dried as soon as possible to prevent permanent damage.

Sickness also hampered progress. At the end of November, on the date of departure, one of the passengers, Liang Sicheng (the famous architectural historian) suddenly developed a fever. For that reason the whole Liang family, including the two children, mother-in-law, and wife Lin Huiyin, had to postpone their departure. Often the passengers had to ride on open trucks, exposing themselves to the elements. Among the travelers there were some as old as 70-plus, while others were babies still wearing diapers.

On December 4, Li Fang-Kuei was put in charge of a bus carrying precious cargo: the families of the Institute of History and Philology, including children and the elderly. When the bus reached Qujing, about 85 miles from Kunming, one of the tires of the bus had a blow-out (*baotai*). No simple flat tire, it was not repairable. Therefore the entire group on board had to wait for a new tire to arrive from the bus company. The busload of passengers was forced to wait an entire week for the new tire to arrive. To make matters worse, it was winter time, and the weather was cold and wet.

Two years and three months later, on March 4, 1943, an even worse incident occurred. A truck loaded down with measuring equipment from Tongji University overturned at Weining when crossing the dangerous Wumeng mountain range, killing all aboard and smashing the equipment.

1940 Life in Lizhuang

With the arrival of the historians, linguists, architectural historians, archeologists, students and professors, the secluded, sleepy little town of Lizhuang suddenly became a thriving cultural center like Kunming. Whereas Lizhuang was the official name of the picturesque town on the bank of the Yangzi River (which has since become a tourist attraction), it was outside of the center of town where all the action took place. The locus of activity was on the country estate of the Zhang family, members of the landed gentry, some three or four miles inland from the town and the river called Lifeng-shancun (Chestnut Mountain Village), more familiarly known as Banli'ao (Chestnut Valley).It was here that the Institute of History and Philology established its headquarters. To reach the site from the bank of the Yangzi River, one had to follow a narrow path, and then climb up about 500 steps, called the Gaoshiti (High Stone Steps) in order to reach Banli'ao. Thus,

Fig.37. Caimenkou as seen in the old days.

Fig. 38. Chaimenkou today, alas!

it was within the confines of the Zhang family estate that the buildings housing the various departments of the Academia Sinica were located. Colorful names were chosen for the three groups of buildings that made up the complex: Tianbianshang (On the Rice Paddies), Paifangtou (The Memorial Archway), and Xinfangzi (The New House). Li Fang-Kuei's new home was located in a cluster of houses called Chaimenkou (The Firewood Gate). Fu Ssu-nien lived in Guihuayuan (Cassia Court); the historian Lao Gan and linguists Dong Tonghe, Li Fang-Kuei, and several other families lived in Chaimenkou; and Dong Zuobin, the specialist in the study of oracle bones (used in divination by the ancient Chinese) lived in Paifangtou.

1941 June 9. Academia Sinica Celebrates its 13th Anniversary in Lizhuang

Founded in 1928, the Academia Sinica, an organ of the central government of China, celebrated its 13th anniversary in Lizhuang. On this special occasion, Generalissimo Chiang Kai-Shek, the wartime commander-in- chief of China's armed forces, made a special trip to Lizhuang to join in the celebration. The fact that Chiang took time out to participate in the festivities, even though China was engaged in a life-and-death struggle against Japan, showed the importance he attached to the Academia Sinica and its work. The Nationalist government took great pains to keep the Academia Sinica

1941年中央研究院成立第十三周年纪念会留影于李庄板栗坳

Fig. 39. Chiang Kai-shek visits Lizhuang, 1941.

running, supplying it with funds and rations of various sorts, including rice, in spite of the dire economic circumstances during war time.

1942: Field work in Guizhou on the Mak and Sui Languages

In 1942 Fang-Kuei and a graduate student/assistant, Chang Kun, began a three-month field trip to the Rong River in Guizhou province. Guizhou was known for its mountainous landscape, inclement weather, and poverty. Traveling in that part of the country was proverbially difficult, and the living conditions were harsh.

First, Li and Chang rode the bus from Guiyang to Dushan, and then took sedan chairs rides to the county seat of Libo. From there they rode on narrow, shallow boats, steered by skilled Miao oarsmen, which could seat only three to five people. The boats, being very light, barely skimmed over the water. As they rode over the rapids, they could hear the rocks scraping the bottom of the boat. Finally, they arrived at their destination: the villages of Shuiyan and Shuili.

While living with the Shui and Dong peoples, Li and Chang recorded their songs and stories. They had two informants in Shuiyan, Wu Tianfei (was from Shuili, rather than Shuiyan) and Wu Ligui. Their dialects, however, were closely related. Subsequently, they were joined by a Shuili informant, Wu Bingzhen.

Fig. 40. Chang Kun as a graduate student, ca.1942
(Courtesy of IHP, Academia Sinica)

All the informants in this region were wonderful singers. Li recalled, "I first recorded their songs, and then I would read them back to the informant as I had written them down. As I read, I would ask him for the meaning. Once I read back the whole song, the exact meaning would become clear." After three-months of fieldwork, the researchers had collected much valuable first-hand material.

While Li and Chang Kun were working on Yang-Huang and Miao languages, his other assistant, Xing Gongwan, was in Yuanyang village, a suburb of Huishui, working on the Zhong language of the Buyi people. After a few days, Li wanted to know how Xing's work was progressing and decided to pay him a visit. The trip took the whole day. When Li arrived, Mr. Xing found out that his teacher had not eaten anything the whole day. Since there were no restaurants nearby, Mr. Xing could only scare up a bowl of coarse rice sprinkled with a bit of pickled vegetables, and a bowl of boiled water. Unmindful of the cloud of flies that covered the rice, Li picked up the bowl, shooed away the flies with his chopsticks, and began to eat.

When he was at home, Li was known for his sensitive stomach, which caused him to suffer whenever the food did not agree with him. However, when he was in the field, nothing distracted him from his work. Hsu Ying compared Fang-Kuei's determination to get linguistic data to the

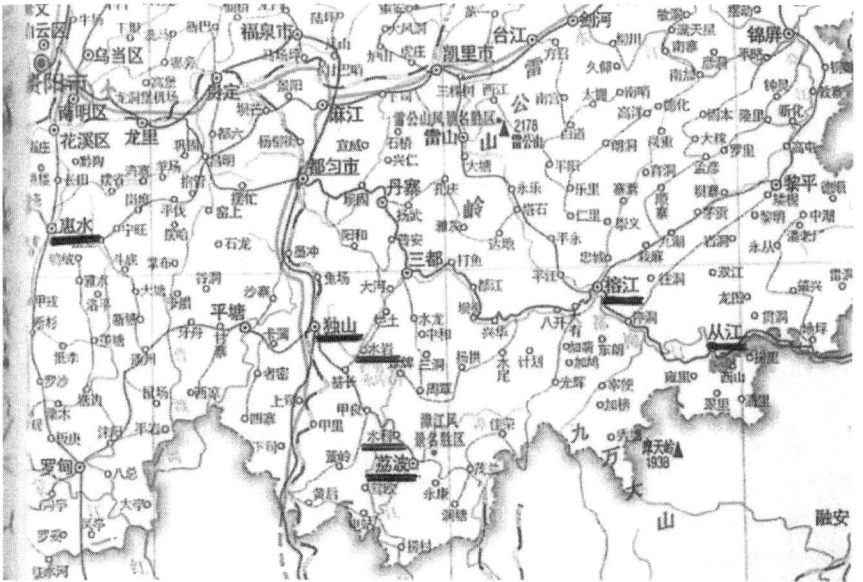
Fig. 41. Li Fang-Kuei's field work in Guangxi, 1942

famous Tang dynasty monk, Sanzang (c. 602–664, or Tang Xuanzang), who went to India to get Buddhist scriptures and had to overcome 81 obstacles along the way.

The complete study of the Sui language was not published until 1977, thirty-five years after Li did the initial field work.

1942 December Fu Ssu-nien Writes to Fang-Kuei Regarding Directorship of the Institute of History and Philology

Fang-Kuei remained adamant in his refusal to assume the directorship of the Linguistic Section of the Institute of History and Philology, causing Fu Ssu-nien much grief. Fu Ssu-nien thought Fang-Kuei was the most appropriate person for the directorship because of his outstanding scholarship and his expertise in training and leading students. But Fang-Kuei would have none of it. Y.R. Chao, who had served as the director of the institute earlier, was away in the United States, and Lo Ch'ang-p'ei did not have the international prestige that Fang-Kuei had.

1943 Publication: "The Hypothesis of a Pre-glottalized Series of Consonants in Primitive Tai"

1) "The Hypothesis of a Pre-glottalized Series of Consonants in Primitive Tai," *BIHP* 11: 177–188。

This article established Li's international reputation as an authority on comparative Tai linguistics.

2) *Makhua jilue* (Notes on the Mak Language). *BIHP, No. 20*, 112 pp.

This monograph was completed relatively quickly, a year after his field work in 1942.

1943 Fang-Kuei Decides to Move to Chengdu

Even though Lizhuang was a peaceful, idyllic, little town, and had become a cultural center, ideally suited for pursuing scholarship and research, it was not an ideal place to raise a family. The weather was hot and humid. The living facilities were Spartan. As the war dragged on, the salary from the government was often not forthcoming, and food was severely rationed. Medicines were hard to come by. Fang-Kuei decided, for the sake of the children and his aged mother, to leave Lizhuang for Chengdu, some 200 miles north, where Yanjing University was. Despite his deep-seated loyalty to the Academia Sinica, which he considered his "home", he had to leave.

In 1943, Yanjing University, the American church-funded institution, was being reestablished in Chengdu after its move from Peking. The president of the university, Mei Yi-pao, was Fang-Kuei's old classmate from Qinghua and the University of Chicago. He invited Fang-Kuei to come to teach at Yanjing University at a higher salary. Furthermore, in Chengdu, being a larger city, food and medicines were much more plentiful. So near the end of 1943 the Li family left Lizhuang for Chengdu.

For the next three years, life definitely improved for the family. Unfortunately for Peter, shortly after arriving in Chengdu, he was diagnosed with tuberculosis and had to drop out of school for three years in order to get more rest and eat more nutritious food.

1943 December 8 Fu Ssu-nien Writes to Fang-Kuei

A grave situation arose when Fu Ssu-nien found out that Li Fang-Kuei wanted to leave Lizhuang for a position at Yanjing University. Fu insisted that Li could not negotiate a change of venue on his own, that he must go through the proper official channels, i.e., through Fu and the President of the Academia Sinica, Zhu Jiahua. Li, on one of the few occasions in his life, lost his temper; he thought that this was a gross violation of his academic freedom. In a long letter, Fu Ssu-nien explained that he had no intention of preventing Fang-Kuei from leaving, but he insisted that it be made clear that Li was still a member of the Academia Sinica and would remain on its payroll in spite of being affiliated with another institution. The leave was to be regarded as a temporary one, even though Li could receive a supplementary salary from Yanjing University. Li was in a huff, and Fu had to defuse the situation. Consequently, Fu wrote a long letter to Dr. Mei Yi-pao, president of the university, explaining to him the arrangement between Academia Sinica and Yanjing University; and the problem was resolved. Li was free to teach at Yanjing University and supervise graduate students, but he also had to be given time to pursue his research projects for the Academia Sinica. Fu was looking out for Li's interest and did not want him to be exploited.

1943 April. Fang-Kuei attends a Conference on the Revision of the Phonetic Alphabet Designed for China's National Dialects

In April 1943 the Committee for Promotion of the National Language of the Department of Education called a meeting of the Committee for the Revision of the Phonetic Alphabet for All of China's National Dialects. Prominent linguists included Li Shaoxi, Wei Tianxing, Li Fang-Kuei, Lo Ch'ang-p'ei, and Wang Liaoyi. They were all invited to the wartime capital of Chongqing for this important conference.

Li Shaoxi called the meeting to order, passed out a thick packet of background documents with a proposal for revising the phonetic alphabet, and asked for feedback. He then left for a dental appointment, saying that he would return in 15 minutes.

However, it was impossible to respond to Li Shaoxi's thick packet of documents within such a short time. Therefore it was decided, under the leadership of Wei Tianxing, that a new table be constructed comparing all the phonological symbols needed for the various Chinese dialects with the standard symbols used for Mandarin Chinese, the official national language. Li Fang-Kuei was given the task of making the summary.

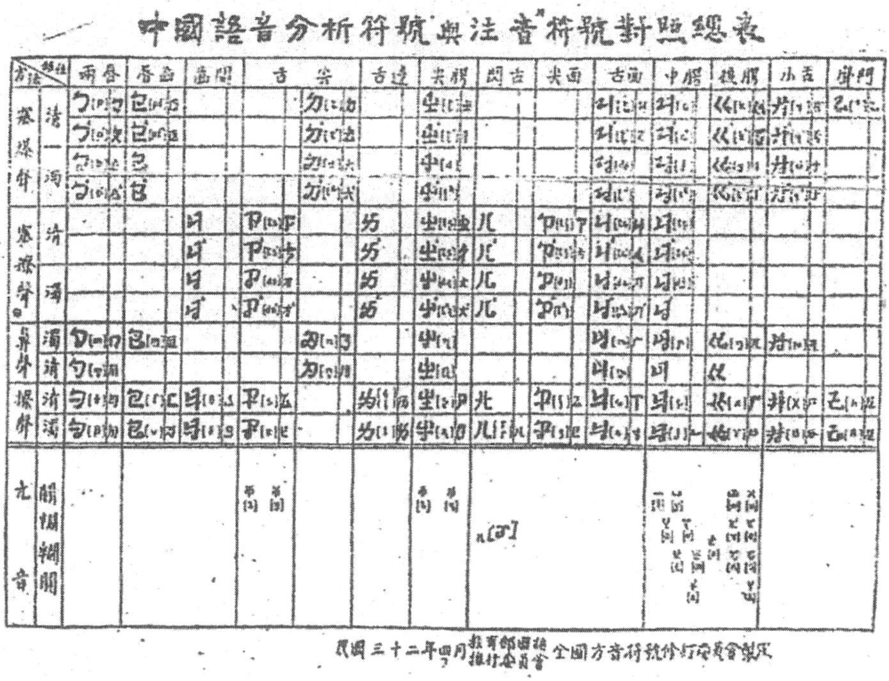

Fig. 42. Chart of the universal system of phonetic symbols used to represent dialects in China, 1943.

Within a mere 15 minutes, Li gave a succinct, systematic analysis of the Chinese phonological system, covering the points of articulation [labial, denti–labial, dental, retroflex, etc, etc.], the 8 different methods of articulation [voiceless stop, aspirated stop, voiced stop, etc. etc.], and so on. At the end of the presentation, everyone was dumbstruck! They had never heard of such a comprehensive and systematic presentation. The audience must not have been aware that Li had already published his systematic classification of Chinese dialects five years earlier, in the *China Yearbook* for 1936. When Mr. Li Shaoxi returned from his dental appointment, he remarked to the group, "Wasn't I fast!" Mr. Wei Tianxing replied, "We were even faster!"

1944 February 28 Fu Ssu–nien Writes to Fang–Kuei

By February of 1944, Fu Ssu–nien worked out an arrangement with Yanjing University with regard to Fang-Kuei's position there. Fu made it very clear that Li's tenure at Yanjing was at the discretion of the Institute of History and Philology and the Academic Sinica. In effect, Li was on temporary leave, or loan, from the Academia Sinica to Yanjing University because of the special circumstances of war. The Li family's household of four plus the two grandmothers was difficult to maintain on government salary, especially in Lizhuang. While at Yanjing, Li was still to receive the limited salary, rice rations, and research funds from the Academia Sinica, but he was also entitled to receive supplementary salary from Yanjing University. Moving expenses from Lizhuang to Chengdu were to be covered by Yanjing.

While at Yanjing University, Li was to be granted time to carry out research; his teaching was to be limited to no more than 5 hours per week. These stipulations constituted proof positive that Fu was looking out for the interests of his highly valued linguist.

1944 June 28 Fu Ssu-nien Again Writes to Fang-Kuei

While Fu Ssu-nien was in Chongqing, the wartime capital of China, recuperating from the stresses of his job in Lizhuang, he wrote an interesting, chatty letter to Fang-Kuei, explaining to him the intricacies of getting approval from President Zhu Jiahua of the Academia Sinica for Fang-Kuei's temporary leave of absence. To win the president over, Fu had to argue that the reason for Fang-Kuei to go to Chengdu was to pursue Tibetan studies. This argument proved to be persuasive because of the existence of a large Tibetan community there.

However, Fu explained to Li that he was under no obligation to study Tibetan; the plan was simply a pretext for getting permission from President Zhu. In the letter he chatted further about the politics at the IHP and mentioned that the two wives were writing to each other. About this correspondence he commented that it would be wise to ignore the advice that his wife, Dora (Yu Dacai), had given to Hsu Ying about finding work to earn extra money. The familiar tone of this letter attests to the close friendship between the two men.

1944 Fang-Kuei Learns to Play the Flute

Hsu Ying had long been a *kunqu* enthusiast; Fang-Kuei, on the other hand, was at best indifferent until they moved to Chengdu in 1943. Since there was not much to do for amusement during the war, Hsu Ying and a few of her friends formed a *kunqu* club that met once a month to sing together. Fang-Kuei just tagged along at first, not showing much interest. However, as time went on his interest grew, and he followed along in the score as the ladies sang.

His interest was finally piqued one day, when the noted painter, Wu Zuoren (1908-1997), came to Chengdu for a visit and wanted to sing *kunqu* with Hsu Ying. Wu, an expert on the bamboo flute, accompanied Hsu Ying as she sang. Fang-Kuei watched and listened intently. Afterwards, he asked Wu about the intricacies of playing the flute. The next day Li bought a flute and had a quick lesson in flute-playing from Wu Zuoren. Wu left Chengdu after a few days, but Fang-Kuei continued to practice on his own, often with Hsu Ying singing along and prompting him.

At first he could not make any sound on his flute, but it did not bother him. He just followed the score, turning pages as he played. This made his daughter, Lindy, jokingly remark,

Fig. 43. Members of the Chengdu *kunqu* club, ca. 1945.

"Dad is not making a sound, but he's turning pages!" However, within a few days, Fang-Kuei's flute began to produce music as he mastered the technique of blowing and fingering for the various keys. Soon he learned one aria and accompanied Hsu Ying at the next *kunqu* meeting. His mastery of flute playing in such a short time amazed all the club members. They could not believe that he had just learned how to play. From then on *kunqu* became one of his life-long passions, alongside his love of linguistics.

1945 Publication: "Some Old Chinese Loan Words in the Tai Languages"

"Some Old Chinese Loan Words in the Tai Languages." *Harvard Journal of Asian Studies (HJAS)* 8: 333–42.

According to Jerry Norman (professor of linguistics at the University of Washington), Li's article is worthy of special mention because it showed the relevance of Tai to the study of early Chinese phonology. Li's examination of the 12 earthly branches (*dizhi*) in several Tai languages revealed a number of very archaic features, going back to a period predating the *Qieyun* (ancient rime dictionary published in 601 CE). This work was admired and often quoted for Li's insights on both the study of Proto-Tai and early Chinese.

1945: Fieldwork in Sichuan with the Jiarong Tibetans

During the winter break of 1945, Li, with his two assistants, Chen Yung-ling and Chang Kun, went to the northwestern section of Sichuan, near the Tibetan border, to study the Tibetan dialect spoken by the Jiarong community. The region was treacherous, making this fieldtrip one of Fang-Kuei's most adventurous ones. The terrain was mountainous, and the Min River showed no mercy. The further they were away from Chengdu, the more dangerous the roads became. Often they had to cross from one bank of the river to the other and then back again. Crossing the river was not a simple matter. There were no brick or stone bridges across the river. The only means across were primitive, narrow suspension bridges (*suociao*), consisting of two metal cables strung across the river, with wooden planks placed across them. Two sets of ropes served as guide rails. On a windy day, the planks were often blown away, leaving only the cables and ropes. The traveler then had to shuffle across slowly while holding tightly onto the rope.

One particularly windy day during this trip, the water level had risen because of rain, and the current was swift. The wind had already blown some of the planks off the bridge. The metal cables and ropes were still dangling across the river. Not wishing to delay his work, Li decided to cross the river without waiting for the planks to be replaced. He took hold of the rope and slowly shuffled across the river hand over hand, while the river rushed beneath him and the wind howled in his ears. His assistant, Chen mustered up his courage and followed his teacher across. Chang Kun, unfortunately, had severe vertigo; after several unsuccessful attempts, he gave up and had to wait until the planks were replaced the next day. Even so, he had to be carried across in a sedan chair! That same evening a peasant tried to cross, but was stranded in the middle because of high winds. Another traveler tried to help, but all he could do was to tie that peasant to the cables so that he would not fall off while waiting for daylight so as to be rescued the next day. Fang-Kuei did not work with the Jiarong materials directly. Instead, he helped his assistant, Chang Kun, to collect the materials he needed for his research project.

1946 Leaves Chengdu for Nanjing and the U.S.

With the end of the war, Fang-Kuei received an invitation for a two-year visiting professorship from Harvard University to teach and participate in a dictionary project. The appointment was to begin in the fall of 1946. Since it was still difficult to make travel arrangements for the whole family right after the war, Fang-Kuei left first by himself for Cambridge. He flew on a military aircraft from China to Honolulu. After arriving in Honolulu, however, he was not allowed to board another military aircraft to fly to continental U.S.A. because of military regulations. He was almost stranded in Hawaii. Fortunately, he had a friend in Hawaii who had good connections, and with his help Fang-Kuei was able to catch a flight to the continent.

Hsu Ying and the rest of the family followed half a year later on the USS General M. C. Meigs. On the evening of February 14, 1947, the ship sailed under the Golden Gate Bridge and docked in San Francisco after 18 days on the high seas. After a cross continental train ride that lasted two and a half days, the family was reunited again. Fang-Kuei drove Y.R. Chao's old 1941 Pontiac to meet the family at the train station. Hsu Ying had been seasick the whole time during the ocean crossing; she claimed happily that she lost 18 lbs. during the voyage.

1946 Jan 1. Fang-Kuei Receives the Meritorious Medal from the Nationalist Government for Outstanding Service During the War Years

On January 1, 1946 Chiang Kai-shek issued a special certificate of honor to outstanding members of the Academia Sinica for their service during the war, among them Li Fang-Kuei. This was so even though Fang-Kuei did not fire a single shot!

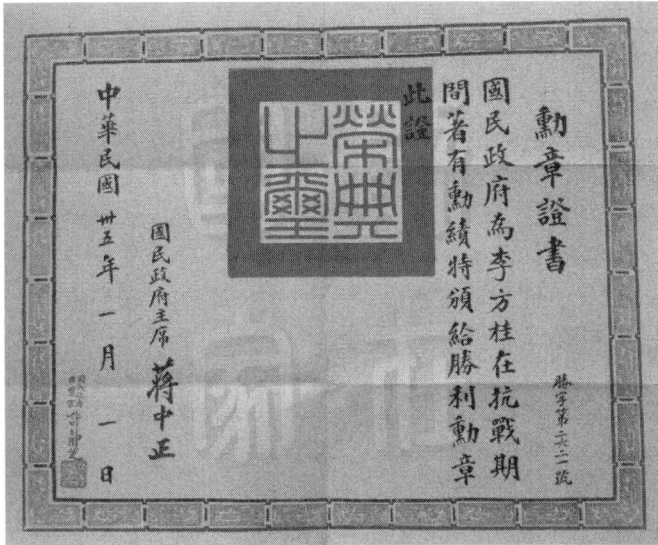

Fig. 44. Certificate of Meritorious Service during the War from
Chiang Kai-shek, January 1, 1946

Chapter VI.

Twenty Years at the University of Washington: Third Trip to America 1949-1969

Twenty Years at the University of Washington: 1949-1969

1946 Back in America Again

When Fang-Kuei arrived at Harvard, Y.R. Chao was leaving for a position at the University of California, Berkeley. To greet Li on his return, Professor Chao left his 1941 Pontiac for Fang-Kuei to drive in Cambridge. Seven years earlier, in 1939, Fang-Kuei had left his own car in San Francisco for Professor Chao to drive back to Yale. The two leading linguists had a perfect working relationship.

After two years at Harvard, Li decided to leave because his work there was not directly related to his research interests. He taught for an additional year at Yale before deciding to return to China. In 1949 Fang-Kuei was honored by the Linguistic Society of American for his outstanding contribution to American Indian and Sino-Tibetan linguistics. He was elected Vice-President of the Society.

1949 October 1 Founding of the People's Republic of China

1949 was a tumultuous year in China. The civil war between the Nationalists under Chiang Kai-shek and the Communists under Mao Tse-dung had been raging for five years, since the end of World War II in 1945. Finally, on October 1, 1949, after the dust settled and the guns stopped firing, the Communist Party under Mao officially declared the establishment of the People's Republic of China. Chiang Kai-shek and the Nationalists retreated to Taiwan. However, even though open hostilities had ended, social and cultural transformations and turmoil continued. The land reform movement and class struggle wreaked havoc on untold thousands of Chinese people.

At this juncture, Fang-Kuei wanted to return to China because he felt that was where he belonged; but Hsu Ying adamantly opposed it. She wanted to give the children an opportunity to grow up in a peaceful environment in America. As luck would have it, while Fang-Kuei was teaching summer school at the Linguistic Institute at the University of Michigan, he received an invitation to teach and direct the Chinese language program at the University of Washington in Seattle. At first he would be a visiting professor for a year. This was to change the whole trajectory of his career. Instead of devoting himself entirely to research, Fang-Kuei now would have to devote a portion of his time to teaching.

1949 Fang-Kuei Joins the Faculty of the University of Washington

The University of Washington was beginning to develop a program in Far Eastern and Slavic Studies and needed someone to build up the Chinese language program. The program directors, Professors George Taylor and Franz Michael, sought

Fang-Kuei as their potential candidate even though he had never been involved with language teaching. But they had the foresight to select him to head the program because of his international reputation. In 1949, after two years at Harvard and a year at Yale, Fang-Kuei joined the faculty at the University of Washington in Seattle.

Beginning as a visiting professor in 1949, in less than a year he was invited to become a permanent member of the faculty. His primary responsibility was to build up the Chinese language program. Even though his training was never in language pedagogy, he took up the task in earnest. He did not take teaching Chinese lightly; in fact, he was heard to have said, the course he enjoyed teaching most at the University of Washington was First Year Intensive Chinese. For the next twenty years, he was in charge of the Chinese language program.

The class began at 8 o'clock in the morning and lasted for two hours, meeting five days a week. As a trained linguist with extensive experience in learning languages, he believed the only way to master a language was through intensive, concentrated study. Not just one hour a day, but two hours a day, five days a week. Professor David Knechtes, who was a student in Li Fang-Kuei's First-Year Chinese class, reflected on his experience:

I most vividly remember him as my first teacher of Chinese. The only first-year Chinese course in those days was a ten-credit per quarter class that met two hours every day, from eight to ten in the morning. Professor Li was a very demanding teacher, who did not tolerate indolence or lack of preparation. I don't know when I worked so hard in a course! Professor Li told me years later that of all of the courses he taught as a professor at the University of Washington, he most enjoyed teaching first-year Chinese. At the time I took his course, I did not know what an eminent scholar he was. It was only later that I discovered that he was the foremost scholar in the world in his field. Yet, he always had time and patience to answer even the most inane questions about elementary Chinese grammar and pronunciation. (Knechtes 1988)

With Fang-Kuei in charge of the Chinese language instruction, Professor George E. Taylor, the visionary director of the Institute of Far Eastern and Russian Studies, did not have to worry about the language program. George Taylor together with the dynamic Professor Franz Michael built up a distinguished polyglot program composed of scholars representing a variety of fields of expertise and hailing from different countries: Helmut Wilhelm (Chinese history, philosophy, and an expert of the *I-ching*), from Germany; Ervine Reifler (classical Chinese), from Hungary; Nicholas Poppe (Mongolian studies), from Russia. Chinese scholars included Vincent You-chung Shih (literature and history), Hsiao Kung-ch'uan (political science and political philosophy), Li Fang-Kuei (Sino-Tibetan linguistics and Chinese), and Chang Kun (linguistics and Tibetan). Other distinguished faculty included Rhoads Murphy (geography), Ma Feng-Hua (economics), Karl August Wittfogel (economic history), and Marius Jensen (Japanese history).

During the time that Li was at the University of Washington, besides being firmly in charge of the Chinese language program, he devoted the remainder of his time to working out many linguistic problems in comparative Tai and Sino-Tibetan. Under Li's stewardship, the university also became a center of Sino-Tibetan studies and Tai languages.

1948 Publication

"The Distribution of Initials and Tones in the Sui Language." *Language* 24.2: 160–167.

The materials for this article were based on the field trip made in 1942 to two villages near Libo in Guizhou some six years earlier. While doing field work in this region Li discovered another language group, the Kam-Sui group, which differed from the other Tai languages.

1949 July 12 Annie is Born

Hsu Ying and Fang-Kuei had their third child, Annie. She was born in Ann Arbor, Michigan (therefore the name Annie), where Fang-Kuei was teaching at the summer Linguistic Institute held that year at the University of Michigan. The University of Michigan was Fang-Kuei's alma mater. It must have been a great pleasure to be back where he studied as an undergrad. Annie was 14 years younger than Peter and 16 years younger than Lindy. She was really the baby sister in the family and brought to it much happiness and liveliness. During the war years, it would have been difficult to raise another child. But once in the United States, Fang-Kuei and Hsu Ying decided to have their third child.

1952 Summer Field Work in Yakutat, Alaska

In 1952, while at the University of Washington, Fang-Kuei took the summer off to go to Yakutat, Alaska, to work with the Eyak Indians. His trip was motivated by Edward Sapir's search for a link between Na-Dene and Tlingit. That link may lie in some Indian languages in the greater Pacific Northwest. Because Fang-Kuei could spend only a few weeks there instead of his usual period of a month or two for fieldwork trips, he felt that he did not do justice to the subject. However, he did publish a short article in 1956 in the *International Journal of American Linguistics* on noun formation in Eyak.

With his customary modesty, Li said, "My work was not satisfactory because it was too short a season for me to do anything, but I hope I did have a smattering of something of Eyak." His colleague, Frederica de Laguna, who also worked on Eyak, disagreed and insisted that he did make a significant contribution.

1954 Publication

"Consonant Clusters in Tai," *Language* 30:368–379.

In this article Li predicted the existence of consonant clusters *tl-*, *tr-*, *thl-* and *thr-* in Tai. At the time, the French linguist, A. G. Haudricourt, regarded this hypothesis as an indication of Li's lack of knowledge about Tai. Unexpectedly, these consonant clusters were later found by Haudricourt himself in the Saek dialect in the northeastern part of Thailand. Later, W. J. Gedney also found *thl-* and *thr-* in the Saek language. Consequently, this article confirmed Li's insight and power of analysis, enhancing his international reputation.

1956 Publications

1) "The Inscription of the Sino-Tibetan Treaty of 821-822," *T'oung Pao* 44:1-99。

This was the longest and most important of the Old Tibetan inscriptions extant and therefore of immense value in the study of Sino-Tibetan linguistics. According to South Coblin, Li's co-author in a 1987 work, "Li's study was unparalleled in breadth, depth, and skill of analysis and elucidation." There were four faces to the stele, which is still standing in Lhasa today. Each face yields important information. The text of the treaty was on the west face in both Chinese and Old Tibetan: the Chinese text written vertically and the Tibetan text horizontally. The east face contained the historical background of the treaty. The north face listed the names of 17 Tibetan officials who took part in negotiating the treaty. The south face listed 18 names of Chinese officials who participated in the negotiations.

Li edited this text as carefully as possible, based on various rubbings. He then prepared a closely annotated, literal translation. Finally, he compiled a complete syllabic index of the text. This study is of monographic length, running a full 99 pages in the journal *T'oung Pao.*

2) "A Type of Noun Formation in Athabaskan and Eyak." *IJAL* 22: 45–48.

This article was Fang-Kuei's final tribute to his teacher Edward Sapir, whose interest in American Indian languages led to Li's study of Mattole, Wailaki, Hupa, Sarcee, Chipewyan, Hare, and finally Eyak in 1952. After a few weeks of fieldwork in Alaska, Li acquired enough materials to publish this article, which led Michael Krauss to note that this was the first time in comparative Athabaskan that anything about Eyak had been written.

1953 Christmas: Lindy's Wedding

Fig. 45. Family portrait Christmas 1953 and Wedding of John and Lindy. (L to R) John Mark, Lindy, Peter; (front row) Hsu Ying, Annie, Fang-Kuei.

1956 May 26 Fang-Kuei Li Teaches at National Taiwan University

During his 1955-1956 sabbatical year from the University of Washington, Fang-Kuei took the opportunity to return to teach at the National Taiwan University in Taiwan and lecture at the Academia Sinica. This was Li's first substantial contact with his old friends and colleagues at the Academia Sinica since leaving China in 1946. It must have been heartwarming. When Fang-Kuei left Taiwan at the end of the school year, the students and faculty at Taiwan National University held a farewell party for him. (Fig. 46)

While at National Taiwan University Fang-Kuei also taught a course on field methods. Afterwards he took two student assistants, Chen Chi-lu and Tang Mei-chun, to Sun Moon Lake region to do field work with the Gaoshanzu.

"Thaoyujilu (Notes on the Thao Language)." With C.L. Chen and M.C. Tang. *National Taiwan University Journal of Archeology and Anthropology* 7:23-51.

1959 Publication

"Classification by Vocabulary: Tai Dialects." *Anthropological Linguistics* 1.2:15-21。

This is another article which becomes part of Fang-Kuei's grand project in comparative Tai linguistics.

Fig. 46. A Farewell Party for Li Fang-Kuei (L-6) at National Taiwan University with faculty and students, May 26, 1956.

1959 July 11 A Visit with the Frankels in New Haven

Professor Hans Frankel and his wife, Chang Ch'ung-ho, were now living in North Haven, where Hans Frankel was professor of Chinese poetry at Yale University. The Frankels, especially Chang Ch'ung-ho, had been personal friends with Hsu Ying and Fang-Kuei since the 1940s in Chengdu, since they were all *kunqu* enthusiasts. Ch'ung-ho, then single, was one of the most accomplished and talented in the art of singing and performing *kunqu;* she always became the center of attention at these *kunqu* gatherings. In addition, she was a poet, painter, and calligrapher. Ch'ung-ho would frequently visit Fang-Kuei's home and occasional attended the *kunqu* gatherings Hsu Ying and her friends organized.

Whenever Fang-Kuei and family were on the East Coast, they would always visit the Frankels to sing *kunqu,* reminisce about the old days, and occasionally do brush painting and calligraphy. In the summer of 1959 on one such occasion, Fang-Kuei wrote these lines of poetry in Chang Ch'ung-ho's guest album. (Fig. 47)

1962-1963 Fang-Kuei and Hsu Ying Globe Trotting

It was not very often that Fang-Kuei took time off to travel for pleasure, but this was an exception: it was Fang-Kuei's sabbatical year. He and Hsu Ying decided to circle the globe this time. They packed lightly and set out on their 9-month

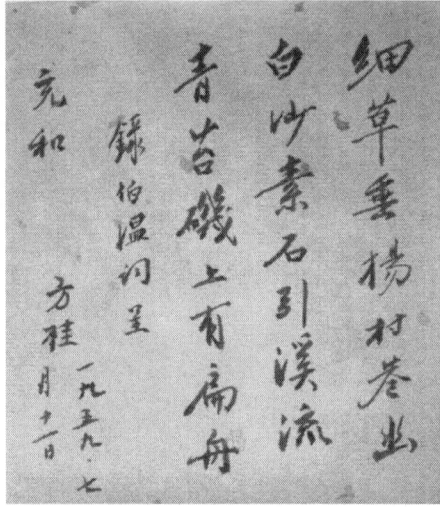

Fig. 47. Fang-Kuei's calligraphy, July 11, 1959

Fig. 48. The Lis visiting the Frankels at 817 Ridgewood Ave.,
North Haven, 1964. Left to right: Fang-Kuei, Ian (on tricycle),
Ch'ung-ho, Emma (on tricycle), Hans, Hsu Ying, and
Peter. Ian and Emma are the Frankel's children

round-the-world tour after attending the international linguistics meeting in New York. They visited the Netherlands, Germany, Austria, Luxembourg, Switzerland, France, England, Italy, Denmark, Sweden, Greece, Turkey, India, Thailand, Singapore, Hong Kong, Taiwan, Japan, and Hawaii, before heading back to Seattle.

Everything went smoothly until they reached India, when their planned fifteen-day stay was cut down to three. According to Hsu Ying, as a linguist, Fang-Kuei felt very much at home experiencing the language and culture of different countries. But he was very frustrated in India because he was unable to communicate with the people even though he had studied Sanskrit for many years.

Another unfortunate experience occurred when Fang-Kuei and Hsu Ying were unexpectedly detained by the police in India. The driver of their motorized pedicab, for no apparent reason, drove the couple to a police station. Later it was determined that because of the border clashes between the Chinese and Indian troops, and tensions were high, the pedicab driver took it upon himself to drive these two "suspicious" Chinese to the police station. The police tried to explain to Fang-Kuei and Hsu Ying that it was a total misunderstanding and apologized for the inconvenience. Even though they were not detained for long, Fang-Kuei felt humiliated and decided to leave India on the next flight. Hsu Ying thought that it was an amusing incident and regretted the fact that they could not stay longer to visit the Taj Mahal and other sights. She also loved and admired the beautiful saris the Indian women wore.

1962 Publication

"*Taiyu musheng ji shengdiaode guansi* (Initial and Tonal Development in the Tai Dialects)," *BIHP,* 34:31-36.

The fifth of a series of ten articles, which Fang-Kuei wrote from 1943-1973 before his *magnum opus, A Handbook of Comparative Tai* (1977).

1963 Publication

"A Sino-Tibetan Glossary from Tun-huang." *T'oung Pao* 49.4-5:233-356.

The Tun-huang (aka Dunhuang) manuscripts, dating back to the Tang dynasty (618-907), were another important source for the study of old Tibetan. The glosses were arranged in accordance with the Tibetan alphabet.

1966 Publication

"The Relationship between Tones and Initials in Tai," *Studies in Comparative Austroasiatic Linguistics* (1966), Norman H. Zide, ed. Pp. 82-88.

A slightly revised English version of the1962 article.

1969 Retirement from the University of Washington

In 1969 Fang-Kuei decided to retire after 20 years of teaching at the University of Washington. It was the same year in which two of his senior colleagues, Professors Nicholas Poppe and Hsiao Kung-ch'uan, also retired. The university suddenly lost three of its most prestigious faculty members. However, for Li it did not mean that he stopped his teaching and research. In fact, he was invited by the University of Hawaii as a visiting professor emeritus for three years (1969–1972), where he continued to teach and write.

During the twenty years when he was at the University of Washington, he continued his research on Sino-Tibetan, Tai, Archaic Chinese, and American Indian languages. He authored over 40 articles, reviews, and notes during this period.

In 1969, Ting Pang-Hsin, one of his later students, was in Seattle for the summer. His office was across the hall from Fang-Kuei's in Thompson Hall at the university. Li's office door was always open, and a constant stream of students and colleagues came by to ask him questions or simply chat. Fang-Kuei always found time to socialize with them. However, as soon as they were gone, Fang-Kuei would immediately return to his typewriter, slowly but steadily pecking away at the keys.

Fang-Kuei's home, first at 215 E. 47th Street and later at 2807-A Northeast 105th Street in Seattle, became the favorite spot for students and colleagues to have a delicious Chinese dinner and a warm reception. Hsu Ying was a gracious host and wonderful cook, who made everyone feel at home. For many students it was home away from home. Hsu Ying's skills in cooking soon led her to start a cooking class and later appeared on the local TV station in Seattle to demonstrate Chinese cooking. Her recipes were soon collected and published in a cookbook entitled *His Favorite*, which became a bestseller and went through several printings.

Fig. 49. A memorable photo of the "Big Five" Chinese linguists
gathered at Fang-Kuei's home in the 1960s at 2807-A NE 105th
St., Seattle. L to R: Dong Tonghe, Li Fang-Kuei, Chang Kun,
Y.R. Chao (with the Lis' cat, Winter), and Chou Fa-kao.

Chapter VII.

Professor Emeritus:
In Retirement
1969-1987

Professor Emeritus – In Retirement
1969-1987

1969–1972 Visiting Professor Emeritus at the University of Hawaii

After his retirement from the University of Washington, Fang-Kuei was invited to teach at the University of Hawaii, Manoa, Oahu where he taught courses in his fields of interest, e.g., phonology of Archaic Chinese, American Indian Linguistics, and comparative Tai. At the University of Hawaii he no longer had to rise at 7 o'clock to teach his morning Intensive Chinese class. This was a great relief to him since he was never an early riser. Life was much more leisurely in Hawaii. Fang-Kuei and Hsu Ying took up swimming and enjoyed the warm sunny beaches of Waikiki where they took a daily dip in the morning. Within a short time, Hsu Ying and Fang-Kuei organized their regular weekly *kunqu* party at their home in Manoa Valley.

One of the students in Fang-Kuei's course on Athabaskan linguistics was Ron Scollon, who later collaborated with him in translating the Chipewyan stories into English including detailed grammatical notes. Scollon wrote about Li's teaching style in the seminar class:

. . . in Honolulu, I took one course from Li Fang-Kuei: a seminar on Athabaskan linguistics . . . I had just completed my first field work on Athabaskan at the Arctic Circle, Alaska in the summer of 1972. The language there is Gwich'in. Edward Sapir had done his fieldwork on Gwich'in with John Fredson . . . he [Sapir] had passed his notes on Gwich'in on to Li. In the first half of the course, Li lectured on historical-comparative Athabaskan. He enjoyed using examples from Gwich'in which came from Sapir's notes. In almost every case his memory of the correct Gwich'in forms learned from Sapir's notes were when he studied them in 1927-28 more than forty years earlier, was quicker than mine, though I had been with native speakers only a few weeks earlier.

In the second half of the course, we began to the study of a specific text in Chipewyan. It was Mandeville's story 19, "How I Made a Canoe." Li began this section of the course by simply speaking the title. He looked at us and, with a gesture, indicated that we should repeat after him. We struggled to do that and then, a phrase at a time, he led us through an oral recitation of the first paragraph of the story. He discouraged us from looking at the printed page while we did this.

Then he told us to go home and memorize the story before the next class. He said it was important for us to have the story "in our ears before we began our closer linguistic analysis." We then worked through the text word by word, morpheme by morpheme, trying to recapitulate Li's explanation for each syllable and each word. A few weeks later he then gave us story 21, "How I Hunted Beaver," which we had never seen before. He had written it out phonemically by hand from his original notes. His instructions were: "Do the same thing on your own." In each subsequent class he checked our analyses against each other's and against his own. (Scollon 2009: 131)

1970 August 10 Li's Visit to the Institute of History and Philology in Nangang, Taiwan

After his retirement, Fang-Kuei had more time to returned to Taiwan visiting his friends and colleagues, and more importantly continuing his research at Academia Sinica now located in Nangang, a suburb of Taipei, Taiwan. He was always a welcomed guest at the Academia Sinica. Students and colleagues often came to visit and to chat. One of his graduate students described Fang-Kuei's typical day: he arrived early in the morning and work through the day until around 4:00 o'clock in the afternoon. Then, he would relax, gather his students and colleagues around him and chat about his experiences working in the field and discuss linguistic issues. Even though the weather was usually hot and humid during the summer months, it did not bother him; he enjoyed the intellectual comraderie.

This photo (Fig. 50) was taken on one of his visits to the Institute of History and Philology in Nangang. A few days after this

Fig. 50. In front of the IHP of the Academia Sinica, Nangang,1970. From left, front row L1 Marjorie Li, L3 Fu Yiqin, L4 Yang Fumian, L5 Chen Xiuying, L6 Lin Yukeng, *L7 LI FANG-KUEI*, L8 Yang Shifeng; back row L1 Liao Qiuzhong, L2 Yu Guangxiong, L3 **Li Rengui**, L4 Li Mingguang, L6 Zheng Hengxiong, L7 Xin Mian, L8 Wu Kuang, L9 Zhang Yiren, L10 **Ting Pangxin**, R1 Lindy Li Mark..

photo, he and Hsu Ying left for Hong Kong to deliver at public lecture at the Chinese University of Hong Kong.

1970 August 25 "The Father of Non-Han Chinese Linguistics" is Born

When Professor Chou Fa-kao of the Chinese University of Hong Kong, invited Fang-Kuei to deliver a public lecture on August 25th in Hong Kong, he introduced Fang-Kuei as "The Father of Non-Han Chinese Linguistics." Some forty years earlier, in the 1930s, Y.R. Chao, received the distinction of being named "The Father of Han Chinese Linguistics" from Fu Ssu-nien for his work on Chinese dialects. Fang-Kuei deserved this distinction because of his more than forty years of research on the application of modern linguistic methods to the study of non-Han minority languages in China.

From this point onward, after 1970, Li Fang-Kuei was always referred to as "The Father of Non-Han Chinese Linguistics." Fang-Kuei's lecture on that occasion was "Initial Consonants in Archaic Chinese." It was subsequently published as "Notes on Archaic Chinese Consonants" in *The Chinese University of Hong Journal of Chinese Studies.* 3.2:511–519.

1971 Publication

"*Shangguyin yanjiu* [Studies on Archaic Chinese Phonology]." *Tsinghua Journal of Chinese Studies, n.s. Vol. 9.* 1–2:1–61,1971.

Translated into English by G. L. Mattos, *Monumenta Serica* 31:219–287. (1974–1975).

Archaic Chinese was a subject Fang-Kuei studied out of personal interest. He lectured on it at times in some of his classes, but did not intend it for publication. Professor South Coblin, one of Li's later students, gave this account of how Fang-Kuei's study of archaic Chinese came to be published:

> . . . *in 1968 he gave a series of lectures on his system at the Academia Sinica and Taiwan National University. These were tape-recorded and the recordings were subsequently transcribed and circulated informally under the title of 'Shangguyin'. From Taiwan copies quickly reached North America, where the newly developed miracle of Xerography quickly resulted in multiple copies. Everybody wanted one. Some of the copies were also acquired by major research libraries and were catalogued under Li's name, as if they were published books. Li was taken aback by this, but it forced his hand in a way that nothing else could have. During his last year in Seattle, he began to write up the material in publishable form and read it aloud as his contribution to the seminar he was teaching. Several years later it appeared in the* Tsinghua Journal of Chinese Studies *and was later published as a book in Beijing."* (Coblin 2000: 374)

S. Robert Ramsey, in his *The Languages of China* (1987) wrote: "Fang-Kuei Li's reconstructions [of Archaic Chinese], in particular, have won praise in recent years for their internal consistency, as well as for their daring and innovative solution to certain problems. However, Li has not yet published a dictionary of the reconstructions [as] given by Karlgren in *Grammata Serica Recensa* [which] remain more accessible to non-specialists."

1972 May 7 Receives Honorary D. Litt. from The University of Michigan, Ann Arbor, Michigan

When Fang-Kuei went to Ann Arbor to receive his Honorary Doctor of Letters Degree from his *alma mater*, the University of Michigan, it was a celebratory moment. On the eve of the convocation his colleagues held a banquet honoring him. Professor William Gedney, a colleague in Tai linguistics at the University of Michigan, rose and remarked:

I am happy to report to you all that tomorrow our alumnus Li Fang-kuei will receive an Honorary Doctor of Letters degree. Dr. Li came here from China in 1924. After two years he received his Bachelor of Arts degree in 1926. Then he went to the University of Chicago where he earned his Master's degree in 1927. And in his fourth year he earned his Ph.D. in 1928. Thus, in four years he earned three degrees. He was indeed very fast. Now finally after a delay of over forty years, we are conferring on him his fourth degree. . ." In conclusion, Professor Gedney added, "*Once his name was mentioned for the honorary degree, 39 letters of endorsement poured*

Fig. 51. Fang-Kuei with Robben Wright, 9th President of
the University of Michigan, 1972

in from many countries around the world including many leading universities in the world . . ."

The following statement from the University of Michigan Honorary Degrees Committee summarized some of his achievements:

After compiling a superior undergraduate record at Michigan, Professor Li attained an early distinction in American-Indian linguistics—an interest of his graduate teacher, the late great Edward Sapir. He subsequently extended his ample purview to the historical phonology of Chinese, to Sino-Tibetan languages, and to comparative and historical studies of the Tai language family. His exact and far-ranging field work, his firm and yet subtle analyses, and his lucid exposition have established his absolute primacy in particular fields of language study and have served as a model and example for linguists generally. Because his scholarly dedication has been selfless, finally, he has been singularly open and generous throughout his career, so that both his peers and his junior associates love him as well as admire him.

The University of Michigan expresses its own admiration and affection for Professor Li as it tenders him the degree Doctors of Letters.

1973 Autumn Visiting Professor at Princeton University

Fang-Kuei was a Visiting Professor for a semester at Princeton University teaching courses on Chinese linguistics. There were many old friends at Princeton; some were former students and now colleagues from the University of Washington, such as Professors Fritz Mote and Marius Jensen. Peter, Fang-Kuei's son, just began teaching at Rutgers University in New Brunswick, New Jersey which was half an hour away. It was a wonderful occasion for old friends and family to get together. Peter and Marjorie's first child, Jennifer, was just two years old at the time, had a great time visiting with her grandparents.

1976 June 5 Fang-Kuei Explains to a Layman What a Linguist Does

In June of 1976, before the publication of his *A Handbook on Comparative Tai*, his then son-in-law, Charlie Bishop, asked Fang-Kuei what he did as linguist. Never missing an opportunity to explain to a lay person what linguistics was about, Li wrote him a letter a few days later, explaining to him what he did as a professional linguist.

Thank you for your interest in my research work. It is difficult to describe linguistic work for a non-specialist. My work consists of (1) to go to the field to record the speech where no previous work has been done. This includes my work in American Indian languages and the Tai languages, especially those unrecorded dialects; (2) an analysis of the language concerned; its phonology, morphology, text and glossary; (3) reconstruction of earlier or proto-language, from which the modern dialects can be derived. This is chiefly what I have been working on in the last decades about Tai languages, and about Chinese. I have finished my comparative Tai work which is in the process of being published. I am presently engaged in writing a study of the Sui language remotely related to the Tai language, chiefly in editing the translation of the texts and compiling a glossary from field material gathered about 30 years ago. I am also a consultant on the study of Austronesian languages in Taiwan, and directing research in the Tibetan language. This is about all I can say just now. (Li 1976)

1976 Publication

Chipewyan Texts, co-author Ron Scollon. *BIHP Special Publication, No. 71.* 450 pp.

This work was 48-years in the making, since his fieldwork with the Chipewyan Indians was done in 1928. Fang-Kuei was waiting for an able assistant to help him put the materials into a more finished form. This person was Ronald Scollon, a graduate student in Fang-Kuei's class on Athabascan linguistics at the University of Hawaii, Manoah. Ron was a resourceful young linguist who had just returned from northern Canada where he worked on Athabaskan languages.

Li wanted to have this material published in its entirety because of the importance of these texts both as documents reflecting aspects of Chipewyan culture and as a linguistic record. However, because of his work with Tai and Sino-Tibetan languages occupied much of his time and attention, he was not able to work on it. Now with more free time on his hands in retirement at the University of Hawaii and with Ron Scollon as his assistant, Li undertook the task of translating and preparing the texts for publication. Four years later, in 1976 *Chipewyan Texts* was published. However, for Ron Scollon this was not the end of the story; he saw the importance of these stories as oral literature. Therefore, he continued to work on them rendering them into literary form and published as *This Is What They Say* (Scollon 2009).

1976 December 21 Honorary Degree from The Chinese University of Hong Kong

At the 17th Congregation of the Chinese University of Hong Kong, The Chinese University of Hong Kong conferred on Fang-Kuei the Honorary Degree of Laws for his accomplishments in linguistics.

1977 Publication

A Handbook of Comparative Tai. Oceanic Linguistics Special Publications No. 15. Honolulu: The University of Hawaii Press, 1977.

This publication marked the culmination of over 30 years of hard work on Tai languages which Li began as early as the 1930s. It is considered the standard reference in the field. In this study Li identified over 1200 cognates in the Tai languages and successfully demonstrated that the standard comparative method can be applied to the study of tonal, non-inflectional languages, such as Tai, in the reconstruction of proto-Tai.

This was Fang-Kuei's most significant work and defined him as the master in the field of comparative Tai linguistics. In tribute to his teachers, the dedication in the book read: "In Memory of My Teachers Leonard Bloomfield, Carl Darling Buck, Edward Sapir" indicating his academic lineage and indebtedness. According to fellow linguist, Robert Austerlitz: "These three names also describe Li's profile as a thinking, working scholar: caution and precision, breadth and depth, imagination and unity." (Austerlitz 1989)

1977 Publication

Suihua yanjiu (A Study of the Sui Language: Texts and Translations). BIHP Special Vol. No. 73, 285 pp.

Going back thirty-five years to 1942 was the time when the fieldwork for this publication was done. Fang-Kuei and his assistants ventured into the remote parts of Guangxi province, to the villages of Shuili and Shuiyan, in the vicinity of the city of Libo, to gather materials for this study. Today the language is almost extinct making this publication more significant.

1977 Summer Herman Collitz Professorship

This year Li Fang-Kuei was designated the Chair Professor of the Herman Collitz Professorship at the University of Hawaii. This chair professorship had been an honor awarded only to linguists specializing in Indo-European linguistics. This tradition was unbroken until it was awarded to Fang-Kuei, whose accomplishments in the fields of Athabaskan languages, Archaic Chinese phonology, and Tai linguistics could not be left unrecognized by the university. On this occasion, Fang-Kuei gave a public lecture on "Laryngeal Features and Tone Change" at the Linguistic Institute held at the University of Hawaii, Manoah.

1978 August First Visit to China Since 1946

After a thirty-two years absence from China, since 1946, Fang-Kuei finally made his first return trip to China at the age of 76. He was urged to make the visit by two letters from China, one from his older sister, Dr. Irene Yi Li (a pathologist), whom he had not heard from or seen in decades; and the other, from his former student Professor Zhou Dafu, a linguist and member of the Academy of Social Sciences.

As a consequence of these two letters, on August 25, 1978 Fang-Kuei and Hsu Ying flew to Beijing, China. They were accompanied by Lindy Li Mark, their daughter and her husband, Dr. John Mark. Being the modest and private person that he was, Fang-Kuei tried to keep a low profile; he did not want his visit to become a political one. He wanted to shun meetings with politicians and avoid banquets. He only wanted to meet with old friends and relatives and do some sightseeing. Of course, given his international reputation, this was not possible; so

Fang-Kuei had to compromise and met several dignitaries and attended some banquets. He led the family through old sections of Beijing, pointing out landmarks here and there which even the guides did not know about. Against the advice of his driver who wanted his guests to see only the new Beijing, Fang-Kuei made a nostalgic visit to his old home at No. 9 Great Sweetwater Well Street which had been converted into a school.

He stayed in Beijing for about two weeks, gave two public lectures on Chinese linguistics at Beijing University to overflowing audiences on September 6th and 7th. During the first lecture, the lecture room had to be changed twice to accommodate the crowd. Finally, a PA system had to be set up in an adjacent room to accommodate those standing outside.

After leaving Beijing, Fang-Kuei and his party, traveled to Xi'an, Loyang, Nanjing, Hangzhou, Shanghai, and finally Guangzhou where he gave a public lecture at Zhongshan University [Sun Yatsen University] where the Academia Sinica had its beginnings. They left Guangzhou on September 23rd after almost a month-long stay in China.

Fig. 52. Fang-Kuei and Hsu Ying revisiting Fang-Kuei's
old home at Sweetwater Well Street in 1978

Fig. 53. By the front gate of #9 Great Sweetwater
Well Street in Beijing, 1978.

1980 August 15-17 The Academia Sinica Holds its First International Sinological Conference

Fang-Kuei was invited to be the Secretary-General of the First International Sinological Conference sponsored by the Academia Sinica. Li, who had consistently shied away from any administrative post, was finally persuaded to take the position by the President of Academia Sinica, Dr. Ch'ien Ssu-liang. This was one of the very few occasions when he succumbed to public pressure. He accepted on condition that he would be given all the administrative support necessary, and he had the able assistance of his former student, Ting Pang-Hsin, who was then head of the Institute of History and Philology. Fang-Kuei's presence was thought to be essential because of his international reputation, scholarly accomplishments, and life-long commitment to the Academia Sinica.

After months of preparation, the conference finally took place and turned out to be an unprecedented success. There were more than 300 participants from all over the world giving papers in six concurrent sessions: 1) Language and Literature, 2) History and Archeology, 3) Folk Traditions and Culture, 4) Thought and Philosophy, 5) Literature, and 6) Art History. The conference proceedings were published in nine volumes containing a total of 280 academic articles.

1982 August 21 Golden Anniversary in Honolulu, Hawaii

This was a happy occasion for the Li family. Fang-Kuei celebrated his 80th birthday after having just recovered from heart surgery six months before. And Hsu Ying had just recovered from surgery for colon cancer. So, August 21 was a very special Golden Anniversary celebration! The whole Li clan from far and near got together. Peter and his family flew in from New Jersey with the grandchildren, Jennifer and Caroline; Annie and Charlie Bishop from Seattle with Robbie; Lindy and John Mark from California with Steven all converged on Honolulu, Hawaii. There were 80 guests altogether at the Golden Anniversary celebration seated at eight tables. Many rose to speak and congratulate the happy couple. Finally, Hsu Ying expressed her thanks to all, and as usual, her words were of benefit all:

Today all of you came here to celebrate the eightieth birthday of one of us and our Golden Anniversary. It is a very happy occasion when one can live up to 80 years old and still be lively and healthy. However, with the marvelous medicine and the unbelievable techniques that physicians have nowadays, it is not as hard to live to an old age. All of us here, I'm sure, will live to 80 and some maybe to 100!

The important and lucky thing is that we recovered quickly from our illnesses. All of you know that we were so seriously sick at the same time. Our three children and our son-in-law came back to take care of us. They all stayed during our operations. But they had to go back to their work even though we were far from being fully recovered. They all left with tearful eyes and heavy hearts. Our great comfort to them was that we have all our good, kind friends and my grandson, Steven, here to take care of us. A friend in need is a friend indeed.

Five months have gone smoothly by. We are recovered about 95%. Now all our children are back with their families for this celebration. This is truly an unforgettable event.

For a couple to be married and live together for 50 years is not that simple, with different personalities, conflicts in careers, living habits, likes and dislikes. So far I have never seen a couple that did not argue or quarrel. It is quite impossible for two persons to live together without disagreement for 50 years. Nevertheless, if both sides can be a little less shortsighted and less narrow-minded, they can compromise and make life much easier. Time goes by so swiftly. To reach a golden anniversary is not that impossible.

After I lived through this disaster this spring, I realized how valuable life is and how important health is. On top of this is the love of our children, grandchildren, colleagues, friends, students, and grandsons and granddaughters. It is too good to describe. Thank you for coming and for the lovely presents!" (Hsu 1984:45–47)

Fig. 54. The Li clan 1982 celebrating Hsu Ying and Fang-Kuei's Golden Anniversary. L to R: John Mark, Lindy, Charlie Bishop (holding Robbie), Hsu Ying, Fang-Kuei, Jennifer, Marjorie, Peter (holding Caroline). Front row: Steven Mark, Annie Bishop.

1983 Publication

"Archaic Chinese." In *The Origins of Chinese Civilization*, ed. David Knechtes (Berkeley: University of California Press, 1983). pp. 393–408.

This is the non-technical version of his more detailed, "Studies on Archaic Chinese Phonology" published in 1971, considered by some to be the bible of Chinese historical linguistics. See 1971 publication.

1983 August Second Visit to China: A Real Homecoming

Ever since 1978, there had been talk of a repeat visit to China for scholarly exchange. But because of health issues, the trip did not materialize until 1983 when Fang-Kuei finally returned to China for the second and last time. My sister, Lindy Mark, gave a detailed account of this trip:

What had started out as a scholarly exchange expanded into the Li family's quest for roots. It came about in this way. In the spring of that year Professor Lin Tao of Beijing University visited Berkeley and met with me [Lindy] informally to discuss the possibility of inviting Li to China for a series of lectures on linguistics. A few months later, the Chinese Academy of Social Sciences and the Central Institute of Ethnic Nationalities issued a joint invitation for Fang-Kuei to visit China.

On August 14, our group arrived in Beijing and were greeted by members of the Academy of Social Sciences and the staff from their office of external affairs. We were lodged at the Yanshan Guest House in the northwest section of Beijing, a few blocks from the Friendship Hotel. After a day of rest, the staff of the office of external affairs briefed us about our stay. They planned a tight schedule of lectures and seminars, some sightseeing, and several official functions, including a luncheon the following Sunday at Fangshan, the Imperial Kitchen. Then we were to be sent off to our destination, Nanning, Guangxi.

The one short week in Beijing was very disappointing, for we had planned to stay after the official exchange to go sightseeing, visit relatives and old haunts. Dad showed his displeasure by saying nothing, not even a perfunctory thanks for their troubles. Privately he fumed, "So they think they can get rid of me whenever they want, do they?" To save the situation, I met with the staff and insisted that Dad have only one official function each day and be able to rest and relax for the rest of the day. I also issued an invitation to the staff to have a buffet brunch at the Jian Guo Hotel, the most famous hotel in Beijing at the time, the following Sunday. That was a big deal for the Chinese to dine at a newly built Western hotel in Beijing. After the buffet brunch the staff was able to rearrange the itinerary without much difficulty. Dad was not pleased with my efforts on our behalf and refused to attend the brunch. But everyone who came had a splendid time.

With the itinerary satisfactorily rearranged, Dad gave two lectures at the Central Institute of Ethnic Nationalities and took part in a seminar. Then there were the usual, unavoidable rounds of official dinners. The most elaborate was held in one of the private dining rooms of the Great Hall of the People, and hosted by Zhou Peiyuan, president of the Academy of Sciences. Zhou, a physicist, was a classmate of Dad's at Qinghua College. Despite its formality, this was the most enjoyable of the official dinners, since Dr. Zhou and Dad actually had something to say to each other. Mrs. Zhou and Mother conversed about old times. The other guests were also members of the Academy whom we knew, so the conversation flowed smoothly.

On August 29 we were officially received at the Great Hall of the People by Mr. Xu Deheng, one of the many vice chairs of the People's Congressional Advisory Committee. This reception was a press event with photographers and TV crew. We all took turns went up and shook Mr. Xu's hand then seated ourselves on large sofas which were placed too far apart for conversation. The two-week sojourn in Beijing was most enjoyable. In addition to the public lectures and official receptions, Dad had many private meetings and discussions. Many of his students journeyed from far and wide to visit him; many younger scholars felt privileged just to sit at the feet of the author of Archaic Chinese, *the bible of Chinese historical linguistics.*

September 2 – 15 Nanning, Guilin, Chengdu

Our next destination was in Nanning, capital of the Guangxi Autonomous Region, homeland of the Zhuang people, the largest ethnic nationality in southwest China. Fang-Kuei's first linguistic fieldwork on non-Han language in China was the study of the Zhuang languages here in Guangxi. We were taken to visit the new ethnological museum and treated to dinner. The next day, Dad gave a lecture at the Institute of Ethnic Nationalities. After a day of rest and sightseeing, Mom and Dad flew to Guilin.

We spent the first day on a boat going up the Li River to view the karst formations which were mirrored in the river. We rode on a double-decker steamer which disappointed Dad, because he preferred to go by a bamboo raft which he rode on when he was doing field work in the region. We had a table at the head of the steamer with a fine view of the river and the mountains on either side. There were many rafts on the river, some with cormorants diving from the bow, some piled high with water plants plucked from the river bottom by boys and girls diving from their bow. We arrived in Yangshuo early in the afternoon and returned to Guilin by bus.

The next day, we took the plane which flew us to Chengdu where we lived from 1943-1945. Dad taught at Yanjing University there. Our hosts were the Academy of Social Sciences of Sichuan and the Institute of Ethnic Minorities. There were quite a few native Tibetans at the institute and they came to call at the hotel in their native costume, loose-fitting coats cinched tightly at the waist and one arm un-sleeved. While in Chengdu, Dad gave a lecture on the Sino-Tibetan Treaty Inscription of 821-822 A.D. This lecture was not about linguistics, rather it dealt with his reinterpretation of the Sino-Tibetan political relations as the result of his translations.

We spent several days visiting the streets where we had lived and could barely recognize them. Chengdu was a big city to me then, but now the streets seemed narrow and cramped. Shaanxi Street was still the same cobblestone roadway. In 1943 Dad came home from a field trip with a bear cub, given to him by native hunters. I still remember how his rickshaw came into the courtyard loaded with his luggage. His precious notes, and baby bear between his knees. The neighborhood children thronged the yard all wanting to play with it. . . .

From Chengdu we visited Qingcheng Mountain, one of the ten great Taoist mountain retreats. The next tourist attraction was the famous water channels of Dujiangyan built around 168 AD.

September 16-25: Chongqing, Yangzi Gorges, Shanghai.

From Chengdu we flew to Chongqing on September 14. There we would take a boat trip down the Yangzi River through the Three Gorges region. We visited the Sichuan School of Fine Arts and its director, Shen Fuwen. Mr. Shen is the foremost lacquerware artist, responsible for developing this traditional craft into a contemporary fine art. He and his wife were fellow *qun opera devotees and belonged to the same music circle in Chengdu in the 1940s.*

The boat trip took two days. . . . At daybreak we left Baidi, a town at the entrance to the gorges section make famous by the Tang poet Li Bai. The river makes thirty-three hairpin turns through mountains that rise steeply on either side; at every turn the scene changes. Dad had never traveled this route before and wanted to see the famous gorges before a proposed dam project changed the landscape. . . . Just before arriving at Wuhan, the river broadens and the skies darken with the industrial pollutants of Hankou, Hanyang, and Wuhan. . . .

Our host institution in Wuhan was the South Central Polytechnic Institute. In emulation of MIT it had a newly established curriculum in the humanities. One of its directors, Yan Xuequn, wanted to establish a linguistics program and was among those instrumental in arranging Dad's visit. Dad gave two lectures on historical linguistics. I was asked to report on anthropology.

From Wuhan, they flew to Shanghai on September 25 where Dad gave a lecture at Fudan University. They again met their old friend, Dr. Zhu Henian, retired director of the military hospital in Shanghai and his wife. . . . From Shanghai they went to Nanjing where they were reunited with Professor Zhang Yuzhe, the late director of the Institute of Astronomy of the Academy of Sciences and his wife. Both Dr. Zhu and Professor Zhang, like

Fifth Uncle Ho, were Dad's buddies from college days. When Dad was with them, they joked and laughed like college kids. In their chosen professions, they spliced the spirit of Chinese traditional learning onto Western science and humanities.

Dad and Mother returned to Beijing on November 6 where they spend a month as guest of Beijing University. During that month, they explored every corner of the Beijing they had known. They saw many friends who were bypassed earlier. Mother's journal was full of names of persons and place names. Dad never kept a journal, but from their remarks to each other, it is quite clear that for Dad as well as for Mother this month was the real homecoming." (Li 1988:128-137)

1984 October 2 Edward Sapir Centennial at the Victoria Memorial Museum, Ottawa, Canada

A group of Edward Sapir's students were invited to Ottawa, Canada to take part in Edward Sapir's centennial celebration from October 1-3, 1984. The participants, Frederica de Laguna, Edgar Siskin, Fred Eggan, Fang-Kuei Li, Mary Haas, and Kenneth Pike were invited to make presentations on this special occasion. Li was one of Sapir's earliest students from his Chicago days. It was here that Fang-Kuei, who was at the mature age of 82, gave some of his most detailed recollection of his relations with Edward Sapir.

When I think back about the things that I studied, I find those are the things Sapir constantly asked me to read about.

185

He gave me important works to read on Chinese phonology, on Vietnamese, and also asked me to read some Thai texts and reader, and asked me to read a Tibetan grammar, and gave me a Tibetan dictionary to work with. These all in the short two years I was in Chicago. I recalled that all these things I later was doing – apparently he started me in all these things that I have been laboring on for the rest of my life, about 60 years of my life. So I wish to acknowledge here the tremendous influence he had on me, not only in the American Indian languages but in many other problems . . . (Cowan, 383–384)

1985 August 26 Receives Award from Chulalongkorn University, Thailand

After a half century of diligence, dedication, and meticulous scholarship, in 1977 Fang-Kuei published his *magnum opus*, modestly titled *A Handbook of Comparative Tai*. Seven years later, on August 26, 1985, Chulalongkorn University, Thailand's most prestigious university, recognized his contribution to the study of Tai Linguistics. He was honored with an award for his Outstanding Achievement and Dedication to the Field of Historical and Comparative Tai Linguistics.

Chulalongkorn University Vice Rector Ambassador

Fig. 55. A Happy moment for Fang-Kuei being
Honored in Thailand, 1985

皇
妙
長
公
主

Fig. 56. Li received by Her Highness Princess
Maha Chakri Sirindhorn (seated right)

Chulalongkorn University, the oldest university in Thailand, was named after King Chulalongkorn (Rama V), and was established by his son and successor King Vajiravudh (Rama VI) in 1917. It combined the Royal Pages School and the College of Medicine. On this special occasion, Fang-Kuei was received and granted the award by Princess Maha Chakri Sirindhorn, who was also a graduate of the university.

1985 September 16 Letter to Ma Feng-hua

Shortly after he received the distinguished award in Thailand, Fang-Kuei reflected on his long fifty years of hard work on Tai linguistics. In this letter to Professor Ma Feng-hua, a junior colleague in the economics department at the University of Washington, Fang-Kuei mentioned for the first time about the loneliness of his work on Tai and his disappointment that no Chinese students in Taiwan wanted to carry on his study Tai linguistics. However, he did have a number of Thai students who studied with him and became established in their field.

I have studied Tai languages for fifty years, but no Chinese student in Taiwan wants to study Tai languages. But I did have a number of Thai students. Now they are university professors, some have become vice-dean of the humanities, and others have become department heads, etc. In America I have few colleagues in the field. Under the circumstances, all I can do is to silently work away. Fifty years of hard work is not very common! . . ." (Li 1985 correspondence)

1987 Publication

A Study of the Old Tibetan Inscriptions, co-author W. South Coblin. *BIHP, Special Volume #9*. 486 pp.

This was Fang-Kuei's final work on Sino-Tibetan linguistics. He began his study of Sino-Tibetan in the 1930s and worked steadily on it until his last days. When he received a copy of this published volume, he was already in the hospital after having suffered a stroke in June. It is the most comprehensive and detailed analysis of Old Tibetan texts available today. In addition to the inscription of the Sino-Tibetan Treaty of 821–822, this volume also includes thirteen other Old Tibetan texts analyzed, elucidated, translated, and glossed by W. South Coblin.

1987 September 21 Fang-Kuei's Long Life Comes to an End

After having been in the hospital on and off for 44 days, initially because of a stroke and later complicated by other medical problems, Fang-Kuei passed away peacefully on the morning of August 21 at 1:45 AM. He had just passed his 85th birthday on August 20th and his 55th wedding anniversary with his wife, Hsu Ying, on the 21st. He lived a long, fulfilled, and happy life.

1988 A Tribute to Li Fang-Kuei from George E. Taylor

When Fang-Kuei retired from the University of Washington in 1969, and when Fang-Kuei passed away in 1987, George Taylor, past Director of the Far Eastern and Russian Institute at the University of Washington, paid tribute to Fang-Kuei in these words:

We were lucky in the China field at the University of Washington. We had Professor Franz Michael, a man of extraordinary energy and ability and driving leadership in interdisciplinary research. It was he who took the initiative in securing Li Fang-Kuei for our team. Among the initial China faculty were Helmut Wilhelm, a Sinologist par excellence who also understood the social sciences; Vincent Shih, a rare scholar of Chinese philosophy, Hsiao Kung-ch'uan, a distinguished political scientist, Rhoads Murphy, a geographer, Ma Feng-Hua, an economist, and Karl August Wittfolgel, in economic history.

In other words, Li Fang-Kuei joined our faculty at a monumental time in American academic history. The motivation to study the non-Western world was very high because World War II had brought our ignorance of these societies to our attention and many academics who had been involved in the war were determined to rectify the situation. One of the most important contributions that Li made in his whole career was to the development of area studies at the University of Washington and at the national and even international level. He modernized the teaching of the Chinese language and his capacity for leadership. He was instrumental in introducing Thai and Tibetan studies.

His hand was as gentle as it was firm. He trained some excellent graduate students, many of whom have made names for themselves, but he also paid detailed attention to the teaching of the language at the undergraduate level. He thoroughly understood and helped to promote the interdisciplinary approach to the study of Chinese society. He was a good team player who even helped, on occasion, with administration. From my point of view as director of the institute, Li Fang-Kuei was a very close associate in a common task. I knew that I did not have to worry about Chinese language and linguistics; most important, I knew that they would stay securely in the institute and not fight for departmental independence. Having all the disciplines together under one roof was essential for the success of the institute's mission. Fang-Kuei more than pulled his weight in one of the great academic revolutions of the post-war period.

Fang-Kuei and his wife Hsu Ying, were the center of a lively and gracious social circle. They entertained young and old over the whole range of the institute. Hsu Ying was the first Chinese woman to offer classes in Chinese cooking. I had the good fortune to be one of her students and am now a constant user of the Chinese cookbook she published a few years ago. The two Li's were the heart of a great family, both domestic and academic.

Dr. Li Fang-Kuei was indeed a very special person and one of the most outstanding members of the institute faculty in the years when we were laying the foundations of what is now the Henry Jackson School of International Studies. The sadness that comes with the loss of a great human being and a great scholar is matched only by remembering with joy and satisfaction and privilege of knowing him. What a reassured block of time it was and what an inner glow we feel just to recall Fang-Kuei's quiet and massive presence. He was a citizen of the scholar of the world, a tower of strength for international scholarly cooperation, a person of great human dignity. He will live a long time among those who knew him." (Li 1988:ii–iii)

Chapter VIII.

The Legacy of Li Fang-Kuei

The Legacy of Li Fang-Kuei

The three men who had the greatest influence on the development of modern Chinese linguistics were Y.R. Chao, Lo Ch'ang-P'ei, and Li Fang-Kuei. They were not only pioneers in a previously unexplored field of Chinese linguistics, they each, in their own way, contributed to the study of linguistics on the international stage. Y.R. Chao was a multifaceted scholar/musician, trained in science and philosophy, contributed to the study of Chinese phonology, grammar, and sociolinguistics; Lo Ch'ang-P'ei, mostly self-taught, worked in the fields of historical Chinese phonology and non-Chinese ethnic minority languages; and Li Fang-Kuei, trained in general linguistics at the University of Chicago, worked most extensively on non-Han ethnic minority languages in China, Sino-Tibetan, Comparative Tai, Archaic Chinese, and American Indian languages.

Li Fang-Kuei's legacy in the field of Chinese linguistics consisted of 1) his large body of writings, over one hundred articles and nine books, which served as models of scholarship in descriptive linguistics for the younger generation of linguists (For the complete bibliography of Li Fang-Kuei, see Ting Pang-Hsin, Bibliography); 2) his concern with data and caution in formulations greatly influenced his students who later became full-fledged linguists themselves; and 3) in 2003, a contingent of Fang-Kuei's younger colleagues founded the Li Fang-Kuei Society of Chinese Linguistics, to continue the legacy of Li Fang-Kuei and Y.R. Chao by encouraging fieldwork and scholarship in linguistics.

Fang-Kuei's obsession with precision and the abundance of accurate linguistic data set him apart from other linguists of his era who tended to do "armchair" linguistics. His theoretical formulations are backed up by hard data, otherwise he would rather remain silent. Therefore, there were no grand theoretical formulations in his writings. Under his guidance and tutelage, there emerged a second generation of Chinese linguists, and they, in turn, trained a third generation of linguists.

Fang-Kuei's concern with data and caution in theoretical formulations had lasting effects on the younger generation of scholars. In the words of one of his later students, South Coblin, at the University of Washington:

A salient characteristic of Li's approach to scholarship was his concern with data. On one occasion I was working with a number of things which for a long time seemed irreconcilable. Then, at last, I hit upon a grand scheme which seemed to encompass them all, and I wrote him a jubilant letter about it. When I saw him somewhat later, he remarked that my solution was interesting and indeed quite ingenious. But then he added, 'Always beware of truly clever solutions to linguistic problems. Avoid them whenever possible. For the real solutions to questions about language are almost invariably simple and require no ingenuity. The difficulties we have with these things are more often than not due to lack of data. If we had enough data, the problems would not be difficult in the first place. Usually, it is better to set a truly vexing problem aside and look for more data than to propound a clever solution.' This story illustrates not only Li's respect for data, but also the other side of the coin, i.e. his strong suspicion of theoretical speculation. Even in the best of circumstances he was leery of theorizing, and in the absence of copious data he had no use for it at all. . . .

In summary, Li's scholarly approach as I saw it was characterized by cautious restraint and conservative skepticism, firm faith in and meticulous attention to data, and a strong suspicion of theorizing which departed to any significant extent from the foundation of a supporting data base. (Coblin 2000:372, 374)

Tung T'ung-ho (aka Dong Tonghe), a second generation Chinese linguist, wrote, "In my writings where I have been strictest in my theorizing I learned from Professor Li. Also don't speculate, and don't say anything, if you don't have enough evidence." Li often cautioned his students and younger colleagues against unnecessary speculation.

Among the second generation of Chinese linguists, Ma Xueliang, who did fieldwork with Li in the 1940s on the language of the Yi ethnic minority, trained a group of third generation scholars including Sun Hongkai, Dai Jingxia, Huang Bufan, and Sun Tianxin who are now carrying on Li's tradition on mainland China.

There are many scholars in Taiwan at the Institute of History and Philology and newly formed Institute of Linguistics of the Academia Sinica who are also carrying on the Li's tradition. Prominent among them, are Ting Pang-Hsin, Paul Jen-kuei Li, Gong Hwang-cherng (1934-2010), and W. South Coblin (professor emeritus at the University of Iowa).

Li Fang-Kuei Society of Chinese Linguistics

In 2002, after a conference held at the University of Washington in honor of Li Fang-Kuei's centenary celebration, a group of younger scholars led by Anne Yue-Hashimoto, Professor of Linguistics at the University of Washington, discussed the need to form an organization to continue Li Fang-Kuei and Chao Yuen-Ren's (Y. R. Chao) tradition of research and scholarship:

Chinese linguistics in the United States began with the work of Chao Yuen-Ren and Li Fang-Kuei; Professor Chao taught at the University of California at Berkeley, Professor Li at the University of Washington in Seattle. Each of them established a magnificent tradition. Now that the Chao Yuan Ren Center of Chinese Linguistics has come to an end at Berkeley, that tradition has been interrupted. A group of scholars who are concerned about the legacy of Chao and Li and who have links to Professor Chao and Professor Li, with Anne Yue-Hashimoto taking the initiative, wish to establish a 'Li Fang-Kuei Society for Chinese Linguistics' as a permanent memorial to Professor Li's contributions to Chinese linguistics and in order to promote the development of Chinese linguistics. (Bulletin of Chinese Linguistics, 1:1, 296)

On October 1, 2003 the Li Fang-Kuei Society for Chinese Linguistics was officially founded and inaugurated with registration of the Society in the State of Washington. The officers of the organization were Professor Ting Pang-Hsin, President; Professor Anne Yue-Hashimoto, Secretary/Treasurer; and Professor Shen Zhongwei, the deputy Secretary/Treasurer. In order to ensure the continued growth and development of the Society, a number of committees were established to oversee the operations: a Committee of Directors, an Advisory Committee, a Development Committee, and Publication Committee.

In 2006, the inaugural issue of the *Bulletin of Chinese Linguistics*, the official publication of the Li Fang-Kuei Society for Chinese Linguistics, was published. Since then a number of conferences have been held, especially to encourage young

Fig. 57. Three Generations of Chinese Linguists at the
Academia Sinica, 1986. From left: Paul Jen-kuei Li, Ting
Pang-hsin, Chang Kun, Fang-Kuei, and Li Yih-yuan

scholars to pursue research and scholarship in Chinese linguistics. It is hoped that the Society will be able to continue the legacy of Li Fang-Kuei by encouraging young scholars to pursue careers in Chinese linguistics.

Epilogue

In writing this chronological biography of my father I have tried to be as objective and accurate as possible. I believe this is how a chronology should be written. Not being a linguist, however, I have not been able to do full justice to his linguistic accomplishments. For that we will need a linguist to step up to the plate. As I continued to write, I felt something was missing. What was he like as person, a father, and a husband? The personal side of him was missing. Therefore, to supplement this chronology I decided to add this more informal portrait of him from my personal perspective.

The following is a slightly revised version of an essay I wrote in 2002, "Vignettes of My Father." When Professor Anne Yue-Hashimoto, to whom I owe a great debt of thanks, first suggested that I write about my father, I hesitated, not having thought much about how to undertake such a subject, but when she went so far as to suggest the title, how could I refuse?

Even so, it was difficult for a son to write about his father, especially for an "unfilial" son who had never taken much active interest in learning more about his father. Although we, his children, were aware that he was a highly regarded linguist and respected by his professional colleagues, to us he was just "Dad" or "Daddy," who, upon returning home after a day at the office, would sit on his big easy chair, read the newspaper, drink tea, and smoke cigarettes until dinner time. Then he would come to the dinner table when called, quickly down precisely two bowls of rice, and return to the living room. He usually did not talk much at the dinner table. He was a man of few words. In fact, this was a family trait: my grandfather was also a man of few words. It was said that in the morning, while lying in bed, he would form the letter "o" with his thumb and forefinger, indicating that he wanted something round for breakfast -- never uttering a word!

My father was thirty-three when I was born, in 1935; he was already a distinguished scholar. Therefore, I never knew him as a struggling young linguist. By the time I came to know him in the 1940s, he had already established himself as a world renowned scholar. My earliest memories of him were that he would be away from home for long periods of time. I had no idea what he was doing while he was gone. This was probably during the time that we lived in Longtoucun, Yunnan province, or in Lizhuang, Sichuan province. As I was to learn later, he was on numerous field trips to remote hamlets and villages to record the languages of ethnic minorities in Yunnan, Guangxi, Guizhou, and Sichuan. While he was away, my favorite pastime was playing in the large courtyard in Banli'ao, Lizhuang, where there was a large, broken rectangular stone tank. This tank must have held goldfish or some such thing in better days. In it

I would find broken pieces of roof tiles or bricks, which I would grind into such objects as a miniature tank, a battleship, or an airplane, natural choices, since it was during the war.

Father's method of raising us was very hands off. He was not particularly concerned about how we were doing in school. He was preoccupied with his own work. Education was more Mother's concern. His philosophy was that you had to find out for yourself what you were good at; no one else could help you do this. Once you dedicated yourself to what you were good at, your future would take care of itself. When Father's students asked him, "What can I do if I study Chinese?" Father's answer was, "If you're good at it, you don't have to worry. If you are not good at it, then you're in trouble, no matter what subject you study."

Father was one of those people who, though born during troubled times and having encountered many obstacles, had transcended them all and triumphed in the end. He had good fortune, a *fujiang* (a lucky general): he was not born with a silver spoon in his mouth, but the heavens were looking out for him. Endowed with natural gifts, he did well in school, made good choices, and was in the right place at the right time. From the time he was born until he was two years old his head never touched a pillow. He was always held. This may account for his good nature. He rarely showed anger, or complained about anything. He never felt compelled to compete with others, nor was he jealous of anyone. He just kept his nose to the grindstone and did what he was good at.

Father was not only a man of few words; he was a master of understatement. Fellow linguist Robert Austerlitz recalled,

In class, Li's manner was so subdued that it was not always easy to distinguish between a simple point of fact or of information and an original insight or a point of unusual significance. I remember and still have my notes of his course on Mandarin Chinese given in 1962 . . . looking at them now, I understand what [Jerry] Norman means when he says that (in 1971) Li was 'reluctant' to accept the then and now prevalent explanation of tonogenesis. Li knew and even avowedly worked with the notion of segmental origin of tones, but he was searching, in his own syllogistic way, for ALL the evidence which would cover ALL the possibilities. Much of what is now taken for granted was mentioned in class in the summer of 1962 but, because of the subdued tone in which it was mentioned, was lost—on me." (Austerlitz 1989, 469)

This description gives the reader some idea of how difficult it was to understand a man like my father. You needed to be constantly aware of the subtleties of his manner and to listen carefully to what he said or did not say.

Aside from his academic accomplishments, Dad was good at all sorts of intellectual games. He was a wiz at mahjong from an early age. Of course it was easy simply to end a hand without any special combinations; but to end up with a good hand, you had to be aware of other available combinations. He was able to hold his own with the best of them. He was also good at bridge, a game he had picked up on his way back from a fieldtrip to northern Canada in the Northwestern Territories. Bridge was one of those intellectual pursuits that father's circle of friends liked to indulge in during the war, when it was difficult just to get a good deck of cards. Father was a much sought-after player in those days in Chengdu.

In the 1950s Father learned to play the game of *go* (*weiqi* in Chinese). With his usual focus and concentration, he got a *weiqi* manual and started by placing the little pieces of white and black stones on the board. After he came home from the office at the end of the day, we would bring his usual cup of tea into his study, where he had set up his *weiqi* board. There he would follow, methodically, the moves in the manual. These games would go on for hours on end—the manual in one hand and the black or white stones in the other. When Mother would call from the kitchen that supper was ready, he did not budge. He was preoccupied with his game. After calling him several times, Mother would storm into the room and flip the board over, scattering the stones on the floor. Then Dad would sheepishly enter the dining room and eat his supper. From this I learned that whenever Mother or Marjorie (my wife) called from the kitchen to come to supper, I was to drop everything and make a beeline for the kitchen table!

Perhaps because of his experience during the war years, or by nature, Father was a frugal person. He did not have any expensive habits nor did he desire any luxuries. He never carried much cash on him. One reason might have been that Mother managed all the finances and ran the household. Mother would give him some money for lunch, which he frequently neglected to eat. Sometimes Mother would tell us to go the office and make sure he ate lunch. When we got to campus, we would often find him in his office, lost in thought. We would then urge him to go to the faculty club to eat lunch. Usually, he would just order a piece of pie and a cup of coffee. Since Father drove his car to and from work every day, periodically he had to gas up the car. Without fail, he would drive up to the gas station and ask for $2.00 worth of gas. He never said, "Fill 'er up." Of course, at that time, gas cost 33 cents a gallon; first class mail, 3 cents; and bread, 16 cents a loaf.

This frugal man, never begrudged us anything. I began to take violin lessons when we were in Seattle; and, as I got more proficient, I needed a better violin than the one I had rented from school. At the time, my teacher was Stanley Spector, a graduate student at the University of Washington, who was working on his Ph.D. in Chinese history. He had a musician friend, Simon Goldberg, who had a violin he wanted to sell. The asking price was $300.00. In those days that was a lot of money. Dad bought the violin for me, even though it must have taken a big chunk out of his salary. It was also during this period of time that he took me to many concerts to hear Jascha Heifetz, Nathan Milstein, Joseph Szigeti, and other outstanding violinists.

When I was attending the University of Chicago in 1955, (following in my father's footsteps some 30 years after his student days), he was a visiting professor there for the summer. He asked me if I wanted anything from Germany, since he was going there to attend a conference. I said off the top of my head, "How about a Leica camera?" knowing that it was one of the best and most expensive cameras around. He didn't say much at the time, but when I saw him a couple of months later, he handed me a Leica! I was surprised and overwhelmed. I used it for many years until it was eclipsed by the new digital cameras. By the way, just recently I bought a small, compact Leica to replace my old one.

In thinking about my father and trying to figure him out, I must bow to some of his former students and younger colleagues, including W. South Coblin, Ting Pang-Hsin, Li Jen-Kuei, Robert Austerlitz, Ron and Suzie Scollon. They seemed to have understood him much better than I did. This man of few words did not open up easily to people. You had to read his mind and be patient. He was generally mild-mannered, friendly, and sociable, but also rather withdrawn. Both he and his senior linguistic colleague Y.R. Chao fit into a similar mold. Both were subdued and men of few words. Their wives, however, were very articulate. These two women might not have been linguists, but they were certainly masters of the spoken language! When our two families got together, you could hear the two ladies chattering away, especially Mrs. Chao, while the two linguists sat quietly, listening. On one occasion that I recall, during a lull in the conversation, Mrs. Chao turned to her husband and asked, "I thought you said you had something to discuss with Fang-Kuei; why don't you go to the study and talk to him?" Professor Chao answered, "We were done long ago!" before tuning in again to the ladies' lively chatter.

Father and Mother were a study in contrasts. Whereas he was a man of few words, she was very sociable, a great storyteller, and a good conversationalist. She always had something to say to everyone, young or old, male or female, a stone-faced academic or the neighborhood butcher. At social occasions, Mother was often asked to say a few words, and she always pleased the audience with her human interest stories and observations on life. When Father was called upon to say a few words, he would introduce himself in a sentence or two and sit down again.

Mother had a good sense of humor and loved to tell a good story or a joke or two. Whenever Mother was in the mood to tell a joke, we would all encourage her. Oftentimes she would burst out laughing uncontrollably before she had finished her story.

Her favorite story was about a fastidious old man, who would go regularly to the barber shop to get his hair cut even though he had only four hairs left on his head. Although we had all heard the story before, when she told it, we would laugh as if we were hearing it for the first time. Her delivery was unique and a joy to listen to. As the late Professor Fritz Mote used to say, "I think Mrs. Li speaks the most beautiful Mandarin I have ever heard." He always wanted to make a recording of my mother speaking; unfortunately, he never did.

As my readers have probably gathered by now, my father has remained somewhat of a paradox to me. He was very close to me, yet I felt that I did not really know him. As I write, I'm reminded of the daughter, June, in Amy Tan's novel *The Joy Luck Club*. When she was asked to tell her long separated sisters something about their mother, she blurted out, "But I don't know her!" Her friends were incredulous: "How can you not know your own mother? She's in your bones!" But June was right in a way. There's a sense of bewilderment when you are asked to talk about someone very close to you. On the other hand, her friends were right too: your parents are in your bones and in your blood. How can you not know them?

It is a complex issue. There are many emotions jumbled together, in conflict with each other. It was difficult to be the son of a famous father. It was not that he demanded a lot from you. In fact, he never demanded much from you at all. But you

209

simply did not want to disappoint him. And that was not always easy because his standards were exceptionally high.

Selected Bibliography

Austerlitz, Robert. "Notes and Reviews: F. K. Li (1902–1987)." *IJAL* 55.4: 468–471.

Chao, Yuan-Ren. Typescript by Y.R. Chao from 1975. Also see Ting Pang-Hsin, "Li Fang-Kuei quanji zongxu (General Preface to the Complete Works of Li Fang-Kuei)."

Chou, Fa-kao. "Yi Li Fang-Kuei hsien-sheng (Remembering Li Fang-Kuei)." *Kuoyu jihpao shu-ho-ren* (People and Books), no. 582, n.p.

Coblin, W. South. "Fang-Kuei Li: A Personal Memoir." See Ting. 367–376; and Li Fang-Kuei Society for Chinese Linguistics. www.lfksociety.org

Cowan, William, Michael K. Foster, & Conrad Koerner, editors. *New Perspectives in Language, Culture, and Personality.* (Proceedings of the Edward Sapir Centenary Conference, Ottawa, 1–3 Oct. 1984). Amsterdam/Philadelphia: John Benjamins, 1986. Pp.371–404.

Dai Jun. *Faxian Lizhuang (Discovering Lizhuang)*. Chengdu: Sichuan wenyi chubanshe, 2004.

_____. *Xiaoshide xueshucheng (The Disappearance of a City of Learning)*. Tianjin: Baihuawenyi chubanshe, 2009.

Hsu, Ying. *Jinhun (Golden Anniversary)*. Taipei: Shi-pao chubanshe, 1984.

_____. *Fang-Kuei yu wo wushiwunian*, zengtingban (*My Fifty-Five Years with Fang-Kuei*, enlarged edition). Beijing: Shangwu yinshuguan, 2010.

_____. *Cuncaobei* (*Sorrow of a Blade of Grass*). Taipei: Zhongwaitushu chubanshe, 1978.

_____. "Kunqu fangyangdaomeiguo (Kunqu Travels Overseas to America)." *Zhongyangribao* (China Central Daily) (11/20/1989).

Hu, Yourui. "Li Fang-Kuei fanguo shangsuyuan—zhenglichuban Yun-Gui fangyan ziliao (Li Fang-Kuei Returns to China to Fulfill a Long Cherished Wish—to Publish his Materials on Dialects in Guizhou and Yunan." *Zhongyan ribao* (China Central Daily), 1975/05/21.

Knechtes, David R., et al. "In Memoriam – Li Fang-Kuei (1902-1987)." Li Fang-Kuei Society for Chinese Linguistics. www.lfksociety.org

Li, Fang-Kuei. "Linguistics East and West: American Indian, Sino-Tibetan, and Thai," an oral history conducted 1986 by Ning-Ping Chan and Randy LaPolla. Regional Oral History Office. The Bancroft Library, University of California, Berkeley, 1988.

———. Personal correspondence with Zhuang Zexuan dated 18 December 1928.

———, Frederica de Laguna, Edgar Siskin, el al. "Reminiscences about Edward Sapir." See Cowan.

Li, Jen-kuei, Peter Li. "Chongfang Li Fang-Kuei xiansheng diaocha xinan shaoshuminzu yuyanzhilu (Retracing the Path of Professor Li Fang-Kuei's Fieldwork with Minority Groups in Southwest China)." *Gujin Lunheng* (Discourses on the Past and Present). No. 29 (2017), 43-56.

———. "Li Fang-Kuei zhuan (Biography of Li Fang-Kuei)." *Guoshi nizhuan* #7 (1998), 129-146.

———. "Wo suorenshide Li Fang-Kuei xiansheng (The Professor Li Fang-Kuei I knew)." *Zhuanjiwenxue* (Biographical Literature). 52.2 115-?

Liu, Shao-t'ang, ed. "Li Fang-Kuei (1902-1987)." *Zhuanjiwenxue* (Biographical literature), 52.4 (April 1978), 145-149.

Norman, Jerry. "In Memoriam – Li Fang-Kuei (1902-1987)." Li Fang-Kuei Society for Chinese Linguistics. www.lfksociety.org

Ramsey, S. Robert. *The Languages of China.* Princeton, NJ: Princeton University Press, 1987.

Sapir, Edward. "An Expedition to Ancient America: A Professor and a Chinese Student Rescue the Vanishing Language and Culture of the Hupas in Northern California." *The University of Chicago Magazine*, *#20* [November 1927]. Pp. 10-12.

_____. Personal correspondence with Alfred Kroeber dated 11 February 1927,

_____. Personal correspondence with Franz Boas dated 9 May, 1927

Scollon, Ron & Suzanne. "Obituary: Fang Kuei Li." *American Anthropologist,* n.s., 91:4 np.

_____. Translator. *This is What They Say. Stories by Francois Mandeville.* Seattle: University of Washington Press, 2009.

Ting, Pang-Hsin, comp. "Bibliography of Li Fang-Kuei Li." See Li Fang-Kuei Society for Chinese Linguistics. www.lfksociety.org

_____. "Chuangxin yufazhan: Li Fang-Kuei xianshengde xueshuyanjiu (Creativity and Development: Professor Li Fang-kuei's Academic Accomplishments." Manuscript, n.d.

_____. "Fei-Han-yu yuyenxuezhifu – Li Fang-Kuei xiansheng (The Father of non-Han Chinese linguistics—Li Fang-Kuei)." *Zhonghuawenhua fuxing yuekan* (Chinese Culture Monthly) 7.8: 1-8.

_____. Anne O. Yue, editors. *In Memory of Professor Li Fang-Kuei: Essays on Linguistic Change and the Chinese Dialects.* Institute of Linguistics, Academia Sinica and University of Washington, 2000.

_____. "Li Fang-Kuei xianshengde laisin (Letters from Li Fang-Kuei)." See Ting & Yue, ed., 377-402; and Li Fang-Kuei Society for Chinese Linguistics. www.lfksociety.org

Wang, Fan-sen. *Fu Ssu-nien: A Life in Chinese History and Politics.* Cambridge, UK: Cambridge University Press, 2000.

Wang Zihe. "Wuti—Fang-kuei dashi guangyaoyongheng (Untitled---Fang-Kuei's light shines forever)," *Guoyuribao* (National language daily) 1987/09/10. P. 3.

Xu Ying, see Hsu, Ying

Yue, Anne. "In Memoriam – Li Fang-Kuei (1902-1987." Li Fang-Kuei Society for Chinese Linguistics. www.lfksociety.org

Zhao, Xinna, Huang Peiyun, editors. *Zhao Yuanren nianpu* (Chronology of Zhao Yuanren). Beijing: Shangwu yinshuguan, 1998.

Zhuang, Lian. "Fu sinian anzhu Li Fang-Kuei (Fu Ssu-nien helps Li Fang-Kuei behind the scene)." *Zhongyangribao* (Central Daily) (1987/09/20). P. 4.

Index

Academia Sinica x, 37–38, 175

Austerlitz, Robert 204

Beijige 69–70

Bo'ai 103

Boas, Franz 23

Bloomfield, Leonard x, 17, 18, 19, 20

Buck, Carl Darling x, 17,18,

Chang, Ch'ung-ho 151–152

Chang, Kun 103, 135–136

Chao, Y.R. ix, 40, 46, 48, 69–71, 94–95, 137, 140, 163, 194, 208

China 179–185

Chou, Fa-kao 163

Chen, Yungling 135–136

Chengdu 126–127

Chiang, Kaishek 119–120, 137

Chipewyan x, 31,33–36, 60, 64, 159, 169–170

Chulalongkorn University 186–188

Cixi, Empress Dowager 2, 4

Clark, Walter E. 31

Coblin, South 36, 164, 195–196

Collitz, Herman Professorship 172

Ding, Shengshu 62

Ding, Wenjiang 48

Duncan, Isaac 27

Edgerton, Franklin 79, 88

Elisseef, Sergei 88

Eyak 145–146, 147

Eureka 24

Frankel, Hans 151–152

Fu, Ssu-nien 37–38, 39, 40, 45, 94, 97, 111–112, 125, 127–128, 130–132

Gedney, William 165–167

Hainan 51–53

Hare Indians 40, 41–42

He, Naiying 4

He, Zhaoying 2, 4, 10–11, 16, 46, 60

Hsu, Dau-lin 55–57

Hsu, Ying 8, 48–51, 58–60, 86–88, 89, 91–92, 176–178

Hu, Shih 58, 81–82

Hupa 24

Jiarong 135

Jiang, Jieshi, see Chiang Kai-shek

Karlgren, Bernhard 41, 61–64

Kennedy, George 86

Knechtes, David 142–143

Kunming 98–99

Kunqu 133–134

Kroeber, Alfred 21, 24

Laocoon 17

Li, Annie 144–145

Li, Guangyu 2, 10, 51

Li, Paul Jen-Kuei xiii, 197

Li, Shaoxi 128–130

Li, Siguang 41

Li, Xilian 4

Lindy, see Mark, Lindy Li

Liu, Xigu 12

Lizhuang 114, 117–119

Lo, Ch'ang-p'ei 61, 62, 128, 194

Longtoucun 99–102, 103–105, 109–111

Longzhou 71–75

Ma, Feng-hua 188

Ma, Xueliang 103, 105–108

Mak-Sui 121–125

Mandeville, Francois 31, 33–36; Philip 36

Marco Polo Bridge Incident 79–80

Mark, Lindy Li 67, 99–100, 148, 179–185

Mattole x, 25, 27, 29, 30, 54

May Fourth Movement 12

Mei, Yipao 126, 127

Michael, Franz 142, 143

Moore, Samuel 16

Mote, Fritz 168, 209

Mukden Incident 58

Phya Damrong 67

Old Tip 29

Pastoral Care 20

Qinghua 13–14

Ramsey, S. Robert 164–165

Republican Revolution 7

Rui, Yifu 114

Sani 105–108

Sapir, Edward x, 17, 18–19, 21, 23, 24–25, 29–30, 33, 78–79, 89, 92–93, 185–186

Sarcee 55

Scollon, Ronald xiii, 33–36, 159–161, 169–170; Suzie xiv

Seymour, Gladys Miriam 91

Shen, Jianshi 64

Simon, Walter 41

Su, Zengwei 71–75

Sun, Yatsen 7

Taylor, George E. 142, 143, 189–192

Tianmulu 76–78

Ting, Pang-Hsin xiii, 155

Ts'ai, Yuan-p'ei 37–38, 45

Tung, T'ung-ho 196

USS General Meigs 137

USS Hoover 83–84

von Holstein, Stael 31

von Hornbostel 40

Wailaki 29, 30

Wang, Shu-lin 11

Ware, James 88

Wu, Zongji 73, 75

Wu, Zuoren 132

Wuming 71–75

Xia, Xuan 8, 10

Xing, Gongwan 112

Xu, Shuzheng 8, 10, 48

Xu, Zhiquan 8

Yang, Shifeng 62, 103

Yang, Xingfo 45

Yao, Xinong 91

Yue-Hashimoto, Ann xiv, 197–198, 201

Zhang, Kun, see Chang Kun

Zhang, Weici 82

Zhang, Yuzhe 12

Zhu, Jiahua 127

Zhuang, Zhexuan 38, 39

Printed in Great Britain
by Amazon